PRAISE FOR BAXTER BLACK

"He could make a dead man sit up and laugh!"
—*Washington Post Book World*

"If I were asked to name a couple of poets who make a nice steady living off their poetry, the names that would come to my mind are Yevgeny Yevtushenko and Baxter Black."
—Calvin Trillin

"Humorist and poet of the ranch and barnyard, Baxter Black has variously been dubbed a latter-day Will Rogers, the dean of cowboy bards, and the Art Buchwald of the Stetson-and-Levi's crowd."
—*Christian Science Monitor*

"Perhaps the most recognizable man in agriculture today is not the U.S. Secretary of Agriculture, not the head of the National Cattleman's Beef Association, not even the point leader in the PRCA. It is, in fact, a mustached former large animal veterinarian and part-time roper who 'just likes to tell stories.'"
—TV Hagenah, *Ag Journal*

"Bax is a great writer . . . a voice from out there that needs to be heard."
—Bob Edwards, NPR

"He sees things that nobody else sees. He has an imagination that is unparalleled."
—Pauline Arrillaga,
quoted by Red Stegall, Associated Press

OTHER BOOKS BY BAXTER BLACK

*The Cowboy and His Dog**
*A Rider, a Roper and a Heck'uva Windmill Man**
On the Edge of Common Sense, the Best So Far
*Doc, While Yer Here**
Buckaroo History
Coyote Cowboy Poetry
*Croutons on a Cow Pie***
*The Buckskin Mare***
*Cowboy Standard Time***
Croutons on a Cow Pie, Volume II
Hey, Cowboy, Wanna Get Lucky?
Dunny and the Duck†
Cow Attack†
Cactus Tracks & Cowboy Philosophy
Loose Cow Party†
A Cowful of Cowboy Poetry

*Included in *Coyote Cowboy Poetry*
**Included in *Croutons on a Cow Pie, Volume II*
†Included in *A Cowful of Cowboy Poetry*

HORSESHOES, COWSOCKS & DUCKFEET

More Commentary by NPR's Cowboy Poet
& Former Large Animal Veterinarian

BAXTER BLACK

THREE RIVERS PRESS
NEW YORK

Published by Three Rivers Press, New York, New York.
Member of the Crown Publishing Group, a division of Random House, Inc.
www.randomhouse.com

Originally published in hardcover by Crown Publishers, a division of Random House, Inc., in 2002.

Printed in the United States of America

Design by Karen Minster

Library of Congress Cataloging-in-Publication Data

Black, Baxter, 1945–
Horseshoes, cowsocks & duckfeet : more commentary by NPR's cowboy poet & former large animal veterinarian / Baxter Black.—1st ed.
I. Title.
PS3552.L288 H67 2002
814'.54—dc21 2002023149

ISBN 1-4000-4943-1

10 9 8 7 6 5 4

First Paperback Edition

CONTENTS

LIST OF ILLUSTRATIONS

FOREWORD

BY HERMAN MELVILLE

Call me unreliable.

It is obvious to all who see my name bandied about that I have been busy writing forewords for legitimate books—Genesis (chapter 7), *The Perfect Storm, On Golden Pond, The Glossary of Narwhales,* and *Who Moved My Harpoon?*

My interest in the sea led me to *Horseshoes, Cowsocks & Duckfeet.* Although I have never heard of this author and have no intention of reading his book, I have always been fascinated by swimming fowl.

Ever since I saw a gravy boat with a duck top and a bowl bottom, I have been curious what they looked like underwater. And, I confess, this led to my study of what cows looked like below the waterline.

I participated in a study wherein I donned scuba gear, took my waterproof Kodak, and sank myself in a stock tank. I waited for the cows to come to water. I was rewarded by the submerged view of posty leg-ged cloven hooves and the squared, rhinoceros-looking lips of cattle slurping water.

As luck would have it, I caught a rare sighting of a watering cowboy who put his palms to the mud and broke the surface with a straining moustache and pursed lips. He rose and fell repeatedly like a lizard doing push-ups on a hot rock. But I diambergress. . . .

I do think cowboys have a lot in common with obsessed, demented, peg-leg sea captains. Both can get intensely focused on besting unbeatable beasts. We are both prone to tangling in the line, getting lost at sea, and spending time with people who exaggerate.

I also think the value of a foreword in a book is highly overrated. Most authors pick someone whose name is recognizable, and this is supposed to lend credibility to the work. I know for a fact the author considered Dave Barry, Salman Rushdie, Zane Grey, Liane Hansen, and Wonder Woman, but none of them would give him the time of day.

So, since I have a lot of time on my hands and am just doing this for the money, take it for what it's worth.

From the *Pequod,* with love,

Herman

INTRODUCTION

This is my third book for Crown Publishers—a division of Random House, a subsidiary of the word-kicker conglomerate, which is a member of the United Nations and working under the auspices of NASA and the Virgin River Hotel Casino in Mesquite, Nevada.

How in the world, one might ask, did a former large animal veterinarian living in the wilds of western obscurity get a book published by a real publisher?

Friends, it is the result of shameless self-confidence, dogged persistence, and shooting arrows into the sky.

In 1981 I found myself down to no keys. Wallowing in the nadir of a bathyspheric existence—my bad luck had peaked. Broke, single, in debt, I was plumbing the depths of my own survival. Like a lizard trapped in a three-gallon bucket.

It was there on my personal seafloor that I decided, since I couldn't sleep, I might as well write a book. I was up anyway. The product of this two-year nocturnal exercise was a novel called *Hey Cowboy, Wanna Get Lucky?* Being ignorant of the process and optimistic in my innocence, I sent copies of the four-hundred-page manuscript to those writers whose words had clung to the cobwebs in my frontal lobe.

I admit, the condition of my life at the time rendered my judgment a little skewed. The lucky recipients were Thomas McGuane *(Nobody's Angel)*, John Nichols *(Milagro Beanfield War)*, Tom Robbins *(Still Life with Woodpecker)*, Dan Jenkins

(Baja Oklahoma), and Hunter S. Thompson *(Fear and Loathing in Las Vegas)*.

Oddly enough, I had also become enamored with Isaac Bashevis Singer, Edgar Allan Poe, and the book of Isaiah, but I didn't have their addresses. As I waited anxiously for a response, I learned the fate of unsolicited manuscripts . . . plywood mostly, or insulation. Yet, one arrow struck a receptive heart. Tom Robbins, that master of Technicolor titles, synchronized writing, and profound philosophy, wrote to me. He quoted my lines back to me. He played marimbas on my ventricles. He said, "You need an agent. . . . Take mine!"

Suffice it to say, my novel was passed around Madison Avenue for a year, got thirty-five rejections, and ended washed up in a box on the shelf in my closet.

Fast-forward to a new life. I had become a raconteur. Without premeditation or intent, I slid down the slippery slope into entertainment. My veterinary clients were gradually supplanted by others inviting me to speak at their agricultural banquet. I became a road man. Then came a new wife and family, a business publishing and marketing my cowboy poetry books, enough money to buy some cows and a used pickup, and a phone call from my agent in 1992 saying Crown was interested in publishing my self-published volumes of poetry.

I declined, thinking, "I sell more poetry books than they do." Not to be deterred, they asked, "Do you have anything else?" The rusty novel, having survived several moves, still sat, in reserve you might say, high in my closet. I retrieved it, dusted off my agent, and it (the book, I mean) sprang to life. Crown published it in 1994, followed by *Cactus Tracks & Cowboy Philosophy,* a compilation of my National Public Radio commentaries back in 1997.

I have been writing a weekly column since 1980. It now runs in 130 papers from the *Delmarva Farmer* to the *Pincher Creek Echo,* from the *Tucson Citizen* to the *Cascade Horseman,* from the *Florida Cattlemen's* to the *Cabool Enterprise* in Cabool, Missouri.

The column is the essence of what I do, which is to "think up stuff." I was admonished in an ancient English class to "write about what you know." My life revolves around animals and the people who care for them; so that's what I write about. It has been said that it is the truth in humor that makes it funny. I agree, and it certainly explains why there are no science fiction jokes.

The stories I write assume a life of their own and, like whining children, continue to pester me to make them a part of something bigger. And some do. They become NPR commentaries or greeting cards or eulogies, poetry books, menu backs, bar sermons, refrigerator art, or even get told and retold in my life performances.

Duckfeet, as we call this book, contains selected tales from the imagination cup that continues to runneth over. They crave attention and this is their chance to shine.

They are, as I describe them, mostly humorous, occasionally political, and accidentally informative.

They are biologically correct, PG-rated, and anxious to please, not unlike the author who is still out there shooting arrows into the sky.

HORSESHOES, COWSOCKS & DUCKFEET

Several years ago I had a job in Baton Rouge, Louisiana. It coincided with my first big loss in the stock market. Thank goodness it was still less than my accumulated cattlefeeding losses or the first divorce. I drove west on I-10 to Acadiana to see if Cajuns were real. I got as far north as Fred's in Mamou and as far south as Cypremort Point on the gulf. I reveled in the culture, wallowed in its strangeness, and was swallowed up by the natives. I forgot Wall Street.

I have returned often. It is one of the few foreign countries I enjoy visiting.

CAJUN DANCE

"Deez gurls ken dance."

He was right. I was flat in the middle of a magic place . . . Whiskey River Landing on the levee of the Atchafalaya Swamp in "sout' Looziana."

The floor was givin' underneath the dancers. The Huval family band was drivin' Cajun music into every crevice and cranny, every pore and fiber, every pop, tinkle, and nail hole till the room itself seemed to expand under the pressure.

The slippers glided, stomped, kicked, and clacked. They stood on their toes, rocked on their heels, they moved like water skippers on the top of a chocolate swamp. Pausing, sliding, setting, pirouetting, leaping from a starting block, braking to a smooth stop, heaving to boatlike against a floating pier.

Then off again into the blur of circling bare legs, boot tops, and bon temps all in perfect rhythm to the beating of the bayou heart.

I have lived a fairly long time. I have been places. I have seen bears mate, boats sink, and Gila monsters scurry. I have danced till I couldn't stand up and stood up till I couldn't dance. I've eaten bugs, broccoli, and things that crawl on the seafloor. I have seen as far back as Mayan temples, as far away as Betelgeuse, and as deep down as Tom Robbins. I have been on *Johnny Carson,* the cover of *USA Today,* and fed the snakes at the Dixie Chicken.

I have held things in my hand that will be here a million years beyond my own existence.

Yet, on that dance floor, I felt a ripple in the universe, a time warp moment when the often unspectacular human race threw its head back and howled at the moon.

Thank you, Napoleon; thank you, Canadiens; and thank you, Shirley Cormier and the all-girl Cajun band. It was a crawfish crabmeat carousel, a seafood boudin Creole belle, an Acadian accordian, heavy water gumbo étouffée, Spanish moss jambalaya, and a Tabasco Popsicle where you suck the head and eat the tail.

My gosh, you can say it again: “Deez gurls ken dance.”

It is difficult to find, except in academic circles, practicing veterinarians who have lost their humility. I think it is because of the company we keep. Animals are not respecters of good looks, intelligence, prestigious honors, or fashion sense.

They remind us regularly of our real place in the food chain.

A COLD CALL

Through rain or sleet or snow or hail, the vet's on call to . . . pull it or push it or stop it or start it or pump it or bump it, to hose it or nose it, to stay the course till wellness doth prevail.

It was a cold winter in southern Michigan: –3°. Dr. Lynn the veterinarian got the call after supper from a good client. Their four horses had illegally gained entrance to the tack room and eaten 150 pounds of grain.

She drove out to the magnificently refurbished, snow-covered countryside horse farm of the couple, a pair of upscale twenty-something Internet millionaires. The three crunched their way back to the rustic, unimproved forty-year-old barn where the horses were now in various poses of drooling gastric distress.

A quick auscultation showed no intestinal movement and membranes the color of strawberry-grape Popsicle tongue. Lynn began her work under the one lightbulb. There was no door, but at –3°, who cares. The Banamine was as thick as Miracle Whip, her stomach hose was as rigid as PVC pipe, and her hand stuck to the stainless steel pump. It was so cold her shadow cracked when she stepped on it.

She pumped her patients' stomachs with Epsom salts and mineral oil. One of the horses, however, did not respond. She instructed the couple to walk the horses while she went up to the house to call the surgeon at the vet school. (Even her cell phone had frozen and would only dial odd numbers.)

As she stepped through the back door of the main house, she remembered that the couple had a pair of Akitas named Whiskey and Bear. Surely the dogs aren't loose in the house, Lynn thought, or they would have said something. She dialed the phone on the kitchen wall. As it was ringing, she heard the click-click-click of toenails on the hardwood floor. Around the corner came a massive beast big as a Ford tractor. His sled dog ruff stood straight up on his neck. The curled tail never moved and the gaze was level. "Good dog, Whiskey, good dog . . . I'm just borrowing the phone here. . . ."

Dogs often remember their vet the way children remember their dentist. Whiskey sniffed Lynn's leg.

"Good dog . . . oh, yes, I'd like to speak to—YEOW!"

The au pair staying with the young millionaires heard a screaming clatter. She stepped around the door to be met by Whiskey dragging the good doctor down the hallway by a Carhartt leg, her arms flailing, trailing stethoscope, gloves, stocking cap, syringes, and steamed-up glasses like chum from a trawler. They were stopped when the phone cord came tight.

"Let the nice vet go, Whiskey," the au pair said in a Scandinavian accent. "She's only trying to help."

The difference between city and country can be as gray as a country-pop crossover hit or as black and white as five-buckle overshoes versus tasseled loafers. But when the twain shall meet, you can hear the rubbing of cultural tectonic plates.

AIN'T SEEN NUTHIN' YET

Mick owned a gas station alongside Interstate 80 in Hershey, Nebraska. It was to supplement his "agricultural habit," as he called his farming operation.

One hot afternoon, a sporty vehicle with Massachusetts plates pulled in to gas up. The driver unwound himself from the bucket seat, stood on the gravel, and stretched. He let his gaze travel the full circumference of the horizon around him.

"My gosh!" he said, somewhat overwhelmed, "what do you do out here in the middle of nowhere?"

"We jis' scratch around in the dirt and try to get by," answered Mick.

"This is the most desolate place I've ever been! There's nuthin' here!"

"Where ya goin'?" asked Mick.

"San Francisco."

"On I-80?"

"Yep."

"Well," said Mick, "you ain't seen nuthin' yet."

Where, exactly, is "nuthin' "? According to Mick, it waited for this pilgrim on down the road. It is 638 miles from Hershey to Salt Lake City, the next city with smog on I-80.

In contrast, I-95 runs 430 miles from Boston to Washington, D.C. In between, it passes through Providence, New York City, Philadelphia, and Baltimore, all of which are bigger than Salt Lake City.

But after this poor traveler got his transfusion in Salt Lake, nuthin' waited for him farther down the road. Picture 525 miles on I-80 west to Reno with nuthin' but Nevada in between.

Some folks say you might see nuthin' on I-10 from Junction to El Paso, or nuthin' on Hwy. 200 from Great Falls to Glendive, or nuthin' on I-40 on from Flagstaff to Barstow, or Hwy. 20 from Boise to Bend, or nuthin' on Hwy. 43 from Edmonton to Grande Prairie.

In my ramblings, I've seen a lot of nuthin'. It appeals to me; breathin' room, big sky. Matter of fact I've seen nuthin' in busy places like south New Jersey, the Appalachian Trail, the Ozarks, the U.P., or outside Gallipolis. You gotta look a little harder, but it's there. Nuthin', that is.

Mick sold the gas station, but he still lives in Hershey. He says it feels like home.

Feels that way to me, too. There's somethin' about nuthin' I like.

Cowboy stories are strewn with wrecks. Horse wrecks, cow wrecks, financial wrecks, Rex Allen, and Tyrannoeohippus Rex. And although one could make them up, it's not necessary. They are a daily occurrence.

WHEN NATURE CALLS

Russell asked me if I'd ever heard of a flyin' mule. "You mean parachuting Democrats?" I asked.

He and a neighbor had hired a couple of day work cowboys to help round up cows on the Black Range in southeastern Arizona. Billy, one of the cowboys, brought a young mule to "tune up" durin' the weeklong gather. When they had ridden the saddled mule through the Willcox auction ring, he'd looked pretty good. But afterward when Billy went to load him, he got his first inkling that all was not as it appeared.

The sale barn guys had the mule stretched out and lyin' down between a post and a heel rope. "To take the saddle off," they explained. "He's fine once yer mounted, but you can't get near him when yer on the ground!"

First morning of the roundup, Billy managed to get Jughead saddled. He had to rope him and tie a foot up to get it done. Then they all sat around for two hours drinkin' coffee till sunup.

As they left the headquarters at daylight, Billy made arrangements to meet Russell at a visible landmark. With all that coffee he'd been drinkin', he knew a "call of nature" was imminent and he'd need help gettin' back on Jughead.

Billy gathered a handful of critters but missed the landmark. By then his kidneys were floating.

The country was rough and brushy. He spotted a ten-foot scraggly pine on the edge of a four-foot embankment. It gave Billy an idea. Not a good idea, but remember, he was desperate and he *was* a cowboy.

He dropped his lasso around the saddle horn and rode up next to the tree. He passed the rope around the trunk and dallied onto the horn. The plan was to snug Jughead up close, get off, do his business, then remount.

The plan went awry.

Jughead started buckin' around the tree on the long tether. He made two passes before Billy lost his dally. Brush and cactus, pine boughs, and colorful epithets filled the air! With each ever-tightening circle, the rope climbed higher up the trunk. The higher they climbed, the more time they spent airborne.

Jughead was hoppin' like a kangaroo when the treetop bent and the uppermost coils peeled off. Mule and cowboy were midair when they hit the end of the line. Jughead went down and Billy spilled into the arroyo.

Almost on cue, Russell came crashin' up outta the creek bottom, "Mount up, Billy. We need help!"

Billy's hat was down around his ears, and he looked like he'd bitten off the end of his nose.

"Uh, go ahead and shake the dew off your lily," said Russell generously. "I guess we've got time."

Billy labored to one knee. "Never mind," he said, "I went in flight."

©2001

Some commentators just can't leave well enough alone.

ONLY EWES CAN PREVENT WILDFIRE

We have long known the sheep to be a two-purpose animal: meat and wool. Now the Nevada Extension Service is finding another purpose: fire control.

Practicing a technique successfully used in California and British Columbia, the Nevadans are using high-density, short-duration grazing to mow the fire-prone grass and sagebrush.

Their motto is "Only ewes can prevent wildfire."

When I first heard about using sheep in fire control, I had a moment's difficulty picturing the scene. Were they flying in low and dropping woolly beasts on hot spots? Were they fitting lambs with gas masks and shovels, then parachuting them into the forest? Or were sheep serving some useful function at the base camp? Waiting tables, perhaps nursing wounds, or simply offering comfort to the firefighters in the form of a shoulder or fleece to lean on?

No! Of course not. The sheep simply eats everything in sight so that nothing is left to burn.

Pretty clever, these Extension Service people. I understand they might apply for a grant to examine other alternative uses for sheep. I've come up with some possibilities they might test.

Need a replacement for the waterbed? Sleep on a bed of sheep. When trail riding or camping, just bring three or four head along. They can reduce fire danger and you can count them at night.

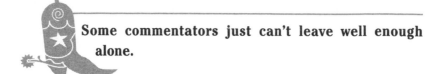

How about soundproofing? When a teenager pulls up beside you in traffic and his hi-fi–whale communicating car stereo is so loud it makes seismic waves in your 7-Eleven Styrofoam cup, you can immediately dial 922-BRING-A-EWE. An emergency crew will be dispatched to the scene and will stuff sheep inside the teen's car until the sound is properly muffled.

Or how 'bout a safety device in automobiles to replace the airbag? In the event of a crash, a Bag o' Sheep explodes from the dash, absorbing the impact, then escapes out the broken windows.

In a hurry at the airport, but don't have time for a shine? Try the Basque Sheep Buffer. Two strong people from Boise drag a ewe over your boot toes, side to side. They glisten with lanolin, and in a hot dance hall when the grease starts steaming, no tellin' what can happen.

Other things come to mind: sheep as large drain stoppers, self-propelled sponges, or a place to store your extra Velcro.

But the alternative use for sheep that may have the greatest potential: Q-tips for elephants.

There are fourteen definitions derived from this story explained in the glossary of this book.

COWBOY VOCABULARY MISCONCEPTIONS

This piece has an agricultural-cowboy slant. However, I am aware that urban people (Gentiles, I call them) read it as well. So when I lapse into my "cowboy vocabulary," I appreciate that some of my meanings could be unclear. Listed are some common misconceptions:

Statement: "My whole flock has keds."
Misinterpretation: Sheep are now endorsing tennis shoes.

Statement: "I'm looking to buy some replacement heifers, but I want only polled cattle."
Misinterpretation: His cows are being interviewed by George Gallup.

Statement: "I'm going to a gaited horse show."
Misinterpretation: A horse performance being held in an exclusive residential area.

Statement: "I work in a hog confinement facility."
Misinterpretation: She teaches classes in the campus jail at University of Arkansas.

Statement: "I prefer the Tarentaise over the Piedmontese."
Misinterpretation: He is picky about cheese.

Statement: "They've had a lot of blowouts at the turkey farm this year."

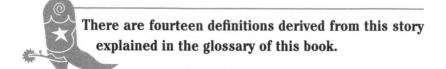

Misinterpretation: Sounds like they better change tire dealers.

Statement: "This mule is just a little owly."
Misinterpretation: His ears stick up? He's wise beyond his species limitation? No, wait, he looks like Benjamin Franklin or Wilford Brimley?

Statement: "Do you know where I could get a bosal, romal, and some tapaderas?"
Misinterpretation: I'd suggest someplace that served Mexican food.

Statement: "I heard that Speed Williams and Rich Skelton got one down in five flat."
Misinterpretation: Must be a couple of quick anesthesiologists.

Statement: "I heard Texas has now gotten Brucellosis free."
Misinterpretation: I assume Bruce, who is of Greek origin, finally got a good lawyer.

Statement: "The Beef Checkoff has gone up to a dollar."
Misinterpretation: Not a bad price for a Russian sandwich. I know the Veal Solzhenitsyn and the Chicken Zhivago are twice that much.

Statement: "You don't have to be a genius to see the team pulls to the left."
Misinterpretation: Whoever they are, they were not satisfied with the election results.

Statement: "I believe that Debouillet has blue bag."
Misinterpretation: She's taken to wearing French fashion accessories.

Statement: "That horse won't break out of a canter."
Misinterpretation: Then that's what I'd keep him in. Beats tyin' him to a post.

Statement: "She's wormed, fresh offa wheat grass, and showin' a little ear."
Misinterpretation: A modest stripper on an organic diet has swallowed her chewing tobacco.

Statement: "You can stick a fork in me."
Correct interpretation: He's done.

COW DISTURBER

McGraw posed an interesting question. If a cowboy herds a herd of cattle, we call him a herder. If a sheepman herds a flock of sheep, he's still a herder. Why isn't he called a flocker?

Oley has always referred to himself as a cow disturber. I think that is an accurate description of what cowboys do. The definition of *disturb* is "to annoy or disrupt."

"Where ya goin', Bill?"

"I'm gonna go check the cows." Which really means "I'm gonna ride into the bunch, git 'em all up, turn 'em around, and just generally annoy and disrupt them."

I grant there are occasions when we have a certain definite task in mind, e.g., "I'm gonna bring in that cow with the arrow in her side." Or, "Saddle up, we're pushin' twenty-six hundred head of longhorns to the sale barn in Bloomfield."

But most of the time, we're just disturbing them. Like doting parents or cat fanciers, we take any excuse to fuss over the critters in our care. It's a wonder whitetail deer or jackrabbits aren't extinct with no one to molest them regularly.

If we were honest with ourselves, our language would be more forthright.

The cattle foreman in the feedlot might give his instructions like this: "Jason, I want you to enter the first pen in the north alley. Unsettle the steers by sitting quietly for a moment. Next, upset them by approaching. Confuse them by weaving back and forth, agitating and irritating them constantly. Badger each one until they've all gotten up and milled around. Once you're convinced you've stirred them up sufficiently, you may go disturb the next pen."

Or, the cowman might say to his wife, "Darlin', while I'm at the board meeting, I'd like you to torment the heifer in the barn lot every twenty minutes. She's tryin' to calve. Peek over the fence and bother her. Shine the light in her eyes to break her concentration. Worry her as often as needed, and when I get back, I'll slip in and frighten her into calving."

In fairness, we are doing what all good shepherds do. We watch over our flocks because that is our calling. We stand guard in case any should need our help. But if truth-in-labeling is ever applied to our job descriptions, we will have to be more specific about what we do.

So the next time somebody asks what you do, try one of these on for size: herd rearranger, bull nudger, sheep panicker, mule cusser, equine perplexer, steer beautician, hog motivator, holstein therapist, cow companion, dog shouter, or cowboy coddler.

HORSE PEOPLE

I would like to talk to you about a certain kind of person that ranks in my mind with duck hunters. Now, don't get your gander up. I'm not gonna say anything about duck hunters. After all, what can you say about someone who gets up in the middle of the night, in the middle of the winter, then goes out and stands in water all day, up to his buckle, and then . . . shoots a duck. But I'm not talkin' about duck hunters, no . . . the kinda people I'm talkin' about are horse people.

Yes, you may have one in your family. You know it when you sit down at the table with a horse person because the first thing they start talkin' about is horses. On and on and on. And if there's two of 'em, you might as well get up and leave 'cause you aren't gonna get a word in edgewise.

And cowboys are the worst. You can be drivin' down the road, three of you in the front seat of the pickup, and you'll pass by this big ol' meadow. In it there'll be fifty-two sorrel geldings, each with one stockin' leg and a snip right on the end of his nose. The guy sittin' in the middle will point and say, "See that one seventeenth from the left, I broke him in 1993." How do you argue with somebody like that?

Or you go out to somebody's place, and they say, "Doc, it's good to see ya! I just got a brand-new horse! I know you'll wanna look at him." See, they think because you're a veterinarian, that you care. Which of course I do!

Well, I have a confession to make: I have come to realize over the years that I have been a horse person all along. I sat there observing, just like you're reading these words, the obsession of horse people with their beast, and I said, "Yes, I know people like that!" never realizing that I, too, was afflicted.

It all came into focus one cruel winter evening: freezing temperatures, 20 mph winds, and snowing hard. Our company had just arrived. I had recently acquired a spectacular King

Ranch gelding. I mean, the brand alone was worth a hundred bucks!

In my excitement I offered, “Listen, I’ve got a really dandy new horse. He’s as shiny as a new Dodge dually, smooth as silk pajamas on a snake, light as feathers on angel food cake, and will eat truffles outta your hand. How’d you like to slip out to the corral and have a look?”

Out of the corner of my eye, I saw my wife display an arched eyebrow . . . a sign of warning. Not unlike the one you see on a teamster’s face when he’s about to take the bullwhip to a wayward ox. You’ve often seen it in Hillary’s eyes.

She calmly said, “Honey, it’s twenty below outside. The drifts are six feet deep between here and the barn, not to mention the fact that your mother is eighty years old. . . .”

The sport of team roping is the cowboy's equivalent of golf. Arenas are scattered across the country like golf courses and many cowboys belong to a weekly roping club. If you have trouble picturing the technicalities of this wreck, it is enough to know that the lasso never comes tight around Kevin's boot.

A FAVOR

Have you ever had a simple gesture of kindness end up unappreciated?

James and Kevin were entered in the team roping and had just chased a steer to the end of the arena in a fruitless attempt to head and heel the crafty critter. James had lost his hat during their run, so Kevin stopped to pick it up for his header.

He hung his loop and coils over the horn and swung off. Well, not quite off. As his right boot cleared the cantle, it hooked the loop!

Kevin remembered very distinctly seeing the rope around his ankle as he neared the ground. He kicked, meaning to shed the snare, but instead, he stuck his toe into Buck's flank!

In that split second, he thought, It's a good thing I'm on ol' Buck. A less seasoned horse would spook. Buck, of course, was thinkin', Whoa! What was that?! He spooked and was goin' flat out in three jumps!

Down the arena they went! Kevin did a couple of half gainers and managed to put a nice figure eight between his boot and the saddle horn!

He sat like a man on a sled tryin' to prise the loop off his foot as he bounced along on his pockets, feet in the air, hands on the rope, leaving a trail through the arena dirt like someone draggin' a sack of watermelons down a sand dune!

Ten feet behind the flashing hooves, Kevin peered through

the flying dirt. They were fast approaching the awestruck ropers at the chute end of the arena!

In desperation, Kevin lay flat on his back and kicked at the captured boot! The loop came loose, his heels bit into the dirt in full flight! They stuck and he stood straight up like Wile E. Coyote runnin' into a canyon wall! With a dramatic flair, he tipped his hat.

James rode by the rigid, unrecognizable figure covered with dirt from his hair to his spurs. "Nice ride," he commented. "Least you could have done was pick up my hat."

Although I wrote this as a silly spoof, there are those who offer animal "psychiatric" services. They have done their schooling in the trenches of telemarketing or carnival barking and have moved on. They are acutely aware that most times it is not the patient who needs counseling but rather the owner. *Nil explota barboocado*. . . . No harm done.

COW PSYCHOLOGIST

"Doc, I've got a heifer that just had a calf. She's not accepting it very well. Can I bring her in for psychological counseling?"

It all started with that call from the worried cowman. My veterinary specialty of cow psychology had gained popularity since my article appeared. It was titled "Paranoia in Dairy Cows" (Doctor, somebody's always tryin' to take something from me!).

I let the heifer get comfortable on the straw.

"Now, Miss Lay . . ."

"Call me Char."

"Char, tell me why you feel uncomfortable with your new calf."

"It reminds me of my past."

"How did you and your mother get along?"

"Same as any cow-calf pair, I guess, although she was pretty high in the peckin' order. It put a lot of pressure on me to achieve.

"Like at the branding. I had to be first! Unfortunately, they let the local banker and the vet rope first. Took forever.

"I remember when I got my horns. A lot of other heifers hadn't started growing horns yet. They were jealous. It wasn't my fault the bull calves thought I was attractive.

"But everything turned sour when they ear tagged me! Yellow! Can you believe it? Yellow! I've never been so embarrassed!

"Then I got a 104 temperature! I felt so left out. I was hospitalized, intravenous injections and everything!

"Finally last spring I met this bull. We made plans. He had a future, had cute rounds, too! I was blind to what was going on around me. I didn't believe the rumors that he'd been seen with other heifers. Then it was too late!

"I had a tough gestation, morning sickness, strange cravings for mint silage and bonemeal. Then I had little Bully.

"I don't know, I guess I'm depressed. Is this all there is to life . . . eat grass, have a calf?"

"Char," I said, *"you're a cow. You've got to accept it. You'll never run in the Kentucky Derby or hunt pheasant. You'll never dance on stage or sing like Reba. Be satisfied with the bovine things you do well."*

She looked at me and nodded. "Yeah, I guess you're right, Doctor." And she left.

As I reflected on Char and my unique veterinary specialty, I realized how lucky I was to have a job that was so satisfying and so easy.

Yup, the world would be a kinder, gentler place if everyone had the IQ of a cow.

BOB BLACK '01

Ah, dog stories. There are books full of them.

MAN'S BEST FRIEND

Talk about relationships: man's best friend, *Canis domesticus, Guardius dedicado, Barkus protectivus, Lickus plateus,* patient listener, uncomplaining companion, eager helper, and therapist substitute.

Have you ever noticed when you leave and come back, it doesn't matter if you've been gone for five minutes or five days, your dog is so glad to see you? Can you think of a single human being that is that glad to see you!

Say you're going to run into town. You jump in the pickup, but you've forgotten the car keys, so you race back in the house. The dog licks your hand, and your spouse says, "I thought you left."

Granted, there are times when *Canis domesticus* becomes *Canis estupido.* Like when you visit a strange farm with your dog in the back of the truck. You are met by a pack of uncivil ruckus-makers surrounding your pickup and barking your arrival to everyone within half a mile.

Your well-mannered beast suddenly forgets that he has been to obedience home school. Forgets all the long patient hours you and he spent together learning to sit, stay, heel, sic 'em, and "away to me." He becomes Goofy, King of the Jungle, engaged in a barking battle when, without warning, his brain comes loose! He leaps from the back of the pickup into the pack of howling farm dogs, and they all disappear around the barn.

But in spite of these semiregular appearances of "good dog dot dom," there are tender moments: like when you've had some assault on your heart or your pride or your satisfied status quo. You walk down by the creek or out to the haystack just to be alone to deal with this new reality.

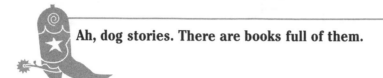

Accompanying you, as always if you let him, is Old Faithful. Head in your lap, paw on your knee, ready to agree to anything you say, ready to soak up a tear or a curse or a sigh. Guardian of your most secret thoughts. Friend without strings, as true as a mother's love, as faithful as Siamese twins, and all for the price of a scratch behind the ear.

People who work outdoors, which includes most agricultural folks, are on a first-name basis with the weather. March, by any other name, would still smell like mud.

MARCH MADNESS

March is the castor oil of months. The collected drippings of winter's oil change. The epic flush of the accumulated compaction of salted streets, sanded roads, gravelly snow, and frozen manure. It is the longest month of the year when you calculate in the miserable factor. March is not a month to expect a kind word from.

It has its own ides. But what ides are they? I can tell you: fungicide, blindside, cyanide, vilified, terrified, stupefied, snide, hide, lied, cried, died, back you up against the wall and leave you flat and down, afoot and weak, and chapped and squinty-eyed ides.

In most of cow country, it is a month to survive. A hold-your-own month. A can't-see-the-barn-from-the-house month. A soggy, windy, coughing, runny-nosed month.

March is how you feel at the end of a three-day hunt in the Bob Marshall Wilderness without a razor, toothbrush, hot water, clean socks, or soap. "I haven't combed my hair for a week. I've been sleeping in my clothes, and I smell like dirty sheets, smoke, and King Kong's sneakers. I feel so, oh, I don't know, so . . . March."

March is the interrogator at the Kremlin, "So, you thought winter was ohfur. . . . You foolish farmer . . . sure you luffed February, Valentine's Day, sunny mornings, happy faces. But you forgot about me! Neffer again!" Then it whacks you with a three-foot snowfall that pulls down entire forests, melts in half a day flooding your pens—which are already saturated—and buries your tractor in a mudslide, blocking the road.

Surely, you say, somebody likes March. Plumbers maybe. Everything is thawing out and breaking. Travel agents like March, selling cruises to the Bahamas to indentured sufferers from Grand Forks, Grand Junction, and Grand Rapids who have enough money to leave. And psychiatrists in Grand Forks, Grand Junction, and Grand Rapids would like March because they service those remaining sufferers who can't afford to leave.

March is like playing tug-of-war with a team of walruses. They don't have to cheat to win. There is no way to beat March. So we just have to let it happen, and occasionally we'll get lucky and it will let us win a hand. We should accept it graciously but never drop our guard. March is not to be trusted.

There is nothing as fraught with impending complications as the comment "This will only take a minute."

SIMPLE PROJECTS

I said, "Shorty, how's yer day been goin'?"

He looked at me suspiciously, like I'd been readin' his mind, then answered, "Where do ya want me to start?"

Shorty's old cake-feedin' pickup had broke down the night before. That meant transferring the cake feeder to his other pickup. "No big deal," he told Maxine. He'd have it done in twenty minutes. It only required drilling four holes in the bed of the new truck to bolt on the feeder.

"Fine," she said. "I'll start supper."

The feeder fit perfectly. "This is gonna be quicker 'n I thought," he congratulated himself. With that, he fired up the drill and bored a hole through the side panel—into the gas tank!

There must be a blank spot in our brain that allows us to forget how often we screw up the simplest project. And the simpler it seems, the longer, more complicated, and more frustrating it becomes.

I laid out my fence line and dug postholes every eight feet. I reached the last hole next to the lane. My gate measured perfect across. About six inches down into that last hole, I hit a root the size of Mount Rushmore. Now the gate looks like a crooked picture frame.

I'm regularly led, unsuspecting and confident, to slaughter. Ignorance of the task at hand probably is my greatest strength. What could be simpler than putting in a drip sprinkler, replacing a starter, wiring a tank heater, cutting your friend's hair, building a feed box, running propane to the bunkhouse, or splicing fog lights onto the new pickup?

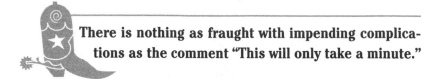

I've been working on my old stock trailer. I bought four new "used" tires. Three lugs broke off the right rear wheel. It took four hours to replace 'em. I rewired the trailer, then backed the pickup close enough to plug it in and test it. It worked! I put up my tools, jumped in the pickup, and pulled away—jerking the wires out clean back to the axle.

It took me all day to put plywood over the floor. I cut and measured, trimmed and fit it to precision. I secured it with ten pounds of drywall screws, then soaked it with linseed oil. It raised the floor three-quarters of an inch. Beautiful job! Now the tailgate won't close. It lacks half an inch of clearance.

CLOTHESHORSE

I'm the kinda cowboy who gives Wranglers a bad name. It's not that I don't try on each pair before I buy them. You have to. You know the old saying about bulls: "There's more variation within the same breed than there is between breeds." Same for jeans: "There's more variation within the same size than there is between sizes."

Maybe I'm just odd-shaped—hard to fit. They do make one style of Wranglers that have legs that fit tight around a shovel handle, which I appreciate. My calves are so puny, I have to tamp dirt in my boot tops to hold 'em on.

But no matter how skinny they make the pant legs, the seat still bags. When I finally do get 'em on, I give the appearance of a swing set somebody tried to gift wrap.

I've gotten picky about shirts. I want buttons, except on the collar, with flaps on the pocket. I kinda back myself into a corner with such outrageous preferences. I can walk into a western store with a shirt inventory large enough for the Chinese army, and the only shirts with my requirements are size 18½-by-32, or they are the spittin' image of a Denny's restaurant uniform.

Of course, style and good taste are not my primary considerations. It's been said that my fashion statement is sort of a cross between Porter Wagoner and Dennis Rodman. I just don't like stuff to fall outta my pocket.

I do manage to wear good boots, which I save for good, but I buy bargains for my work boots. I got a great deal on some steel-toed Red Wings, size 9, on sale for fifty-five dollars. They're tough; I been wearin' 'em for two years. I'm tough, too. I normally wear a size 10.

A good straw hat lasts a year. They've been goin' up five dollars a year, every year. I can remember when they were nineteen dollars. Now they're seventy-five. I'm pretty hard on my hats; they get kinda beat up. My first criteria for a new hat is whether it will come down over my ears and fit tight. Wouldn't want it to blow off during an argument.

I feel like I'm turnin' into a shadow of Ace Reid's cartoon character Jake. Kind of bent-over, narrow at the shoulders. Wide at the hip and big at the hat.

I did some work for Wrangler a while back. They asked if they could pay me in product. I said, "Sure." They sent me a box of Sears, Roebuck jeans.

Large animal veterinary practice first and foremost involves restraint of the beast. Cowboys, ropes, squeeze chutes, shoeing stocks, corrals, fences, good gates, dogs, and all manner of medieval tools and methods have been called into play. Man has been handling these large creatures since their domestication right off the ark. We're still at it.

THE TRANQUILIZER GUN

Except maybe in the opinion of a tiger trimmer in Tanganyika, the tranquilizer gun has not lived up to its potential. During its preliminary promotion, it was touted as the greatest invention since the rope. But, in the livestock business, it has never quite fulfilled its expectations. The biggest problem seems to be its predictably unpredictable results.

Most large animal vets have tranquilizer guns. Some of my colleagues learned the fine art of using one. The rest of us have had it stuck away with our fleams and hog cholera vaccine since 1974. I suspect "operator error" had a lot to do with our failures.

Dr. Green said he and Dr. Corley used it with success when they were gatherin' wild cattle down in Mississippi. It gave them an advantage over better ropers in the area.

Even a good roper has to get within throwin' distance.

The Outlaw family had eight cows and one uncatchable wanderin' bull. The bull was part Braymer . . . the uncatchable part.

Mr. Outlaw kept them in a scrubby pasture next to his neighbor. This neighbor practiced rotational grazing, and his pasture was lush. Mr. Outlaw's bull spent most of his time at the neighbor's. Since the bull managed to crawl back through and breed the eight cows every spring, Mr. Outlaw saw no reason to be concerned.

CAR WASH

When the threats became unbearable, Mr. Outlaw finally agreed to sell his wanderin' bull. He called on Drs. Green and Corley to expedite the matter.

Our boys arrived on the scene, chased the bull back onto the Outlaws' property, and began to trail him through the brush. The bull took a breather in a clearin', and our ballistic vets pulled down and nailed him with the tranquilizer dart. They got him roped and staggered to the open-top trailer, where they tied him in. The bull lay down and passed out.

Mr. Outlaw was pleased: "I'm takin' him over to Bryan Brothers. . . . Oughta get a pretty penny for him!"

"Yup," said Dr. Green. "But he'd be worth more if he walked outta the trailer, fer sure."

"You bet, Doc. How long you reckon it'll take this tranquilizer to wear off?"

"Forty-five minutes to an hour."

"Great! I better git goin'!"

That afternoon, they saw Mr. Outlaw back home at the coffee shop.

"How'd it go?" Dr. Green asked.

"Oh, fine, fine. Made a lotta money. Only had one problem. He was still down when I got there. I had to run him through the car wash twice to get him awake enough to sell!"

Sometimes the difference between cowboy romance and cowboy reality is stark.

CARHARTT COWBOY

Mr. Moses remarked that the other day he'd received a catalog in the mail from a western-clothing outfit. He wasn't sure who the outfit catered to, but the name "Long Island" seemed to stick in his mind.

The photo on the front had burned an image into his brain. A male model stood in cowboy posture, a Clint Eastwood steely-eyed glare glinting from beneath the brim of his Zorro hat.

It appeared that moths had eaten the collar off his shirt.

He wore a duster that was sort of a cross between Jim Bridger's old trapping coat and Santa Anna's parade uniform.

Mr. Moses guessed it weighed more than a wet hallway carpet.

There was an odd collection of gold chains, buttons, military pins, silver boot toe tips, training spurs, and epaulets decorating his wardrobe. He looked like a Filipino cabbie just returned from a Rotary convention.

Mr. Moses imagined himself dressed like the cowboy on the cover of the catalog, jangling out to feed the cows and break ice. Him hangin' his giant rowel and jingle bob on the twine as he kicked a bale off the back of the flatbed. Being jerked flat into the muddy rut, cows tromping giant footprints on the tail of his coat, the dog running off with his pancake hat. Then rising sodden, and trudging off rattling and clanging like a Moroccan bride with a limp.

"Shoot," he said, "I couldn't even walk up to a horse dressed like that."

Mr. Moses considers himself a Carhartt cowboy. For those of you who live in the tropics, Carhartts are warm, insulated canvas coveralls with more zippers than a Hell's Angel's loincloth.

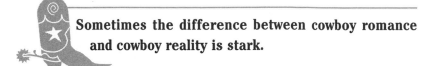

Carhartts, earflaps, and LaCrosse five-buckle overshoes. Real cowboy winter wear. Granted, it limits mobility. You'd have to get undressed to mount yer horse. You can't hear much other than the diesel, but a cowboy can get the job done.

Could be the cowboy on the catalog cover measures his time in the winter by the bottles of brandy he goes through, lacing his evening café au lait; or possibly by the edge of the sun rays on the floor of his glassed-in sunroom. Certainly it would not be by the amount of mud built up in the wheel wells of his Lexus.

Mr. Moses has his own way of judging the length of winter. He says he keeps track by watchin' the pile of ice that accumulates next to the stock tank.

Spoken like a true Carhartt cowboy.

COYOTE COWBOY OBSERVATIONS

- There's always time to pet your dog.
- If a feller doesn't trim his own horse's feet, he's got too many horses or not enough time.
- Some people do what they've gotta do to live where they wanna live. Others live where they have to live to be what they want to be.
- If the reader can't understand what the poet is tryin' to say, it's not the reader's fault.
- Sometimes gentle pressure is better than jerkin' as hard as you can. Kinda like pickin' up a bull's nose.
- The consultant's motto: You can't have all your hands in one pocket.
- People like David Duke and Louis Farrakhan are head and tail of the same bad penny.
- I like a woman that smells like barbecue sauce.
- Some say, "You are what you eat." I say, "You are where you walk. Wipe your feet."
- I observed to a man in New York that I was surprised that they had so many cows and so much farming. He said, "Son, this is where it started."
- The only thing I can't do in excess is moderation.
- It's hard bein' a cowboy. If a man gets run over by a truck, he gets sympathy. If he gets run over by a horse, they laugh.
- You know you had a bad weekend when you wake up Sunday morning and it's Thanksgiving Day.
- A bank examiner is someone who comes in after the battle and shoots the wounded.

- If a person has an excuse to be less than he can be, he probably will.
- Wine doesn't give me a headache. Winos do.
- I felt sorry for myself when I had no hat, till I met a man who had no . . . Wait a minute, that's not right.
- Vet prognosis: Those that linger have a better chance than those that die right away.
- Whoever named the Dumb Friends League has dang sure punched a few cows.
- If you are not generous when you can afford to be, it marks you as a small person. That is not the same as being generous with somebody else's money. That's merely being cheap.

Jack is a real person and just like I describe.

JACK'S CREATION KIT

I can remember the first time I saw Jack. It was then I realized that human beings came in kits . . . ready for assembly.

I appreciate the blessings I've been given: a sense of humor, a good . . . no, uh, a full . . . no, uh, a quick . . . no, uh, a sense of humor. So please don't think I'm ungrateful.

I can watch a good veterinary surgeon C-section a heifer in twenty minutes and admire her. Although it does bring back a surge of memory wherein I'm stripped to the waist on a windy knoll, my knee in the incision to keep the intestines contained, wielding a four-inch suture needle and ten feet of umbilical tape whipping in the breeze. But it doesn't bother me.

I can attend a horse-training class in which the trainer takes a twelve-year-old Belgian/Arab stallion that's never been touched by human hands, and in fifteen minutes, that same horse will be driving a crew cab pickup with manual transmission. As I listen, I see flashbacks of lashing lunge lines, broken poles, steel panels bent double, concrete posts upended, rope burns on the palm of my hand, and the emergency room ceiling. But I'm not jealous.

At rodeos, good ropers effortlessly cast their silken strings around speeding beasts while visions of tangled lines, duckout horses, balky steers, dust clouds, and thumbs the size of Polish sausage flit through my mind. But I feel no envy.

Everybody's good at something, I always say. But when I saw Jack standing on the stage with a guitar in his hand, he looked like a Greek statue of Hercules. Broad across the shoulders, narrow at the hip, tall, a face chiseled from marble, and a full head of hair. Surely, I thought, he can't sing.

He opened his mouth and a deep booming operatic note

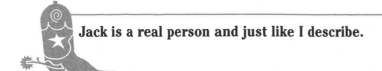

came rolling out. Well . . . the guitar must be a prop. Then he played a rippling set of passing chords up and down the neck. I soon found out he was a magnificent songwriter, sincere, God-fearing, modest, and impossible to dislike.

It was then I realized human beings came in kits. Each kit with equal parts comes trundling down the giant assembly line in the sky. My kit had the misfortune of being next to Jack's.

"Let's make this one special," said the angel in charge. "Let's give him calves like ostrich thighs. Where can we get 'em? How 'bout this box? He's supposed to be a cowboy poet. He won't need calves or shoulders, or hair for that matter.

"Jack needs a voice that sounds like heaven's announcer. We can take most of this poet's vocal cords and just leave him a big nose. He'll get by. . . ."

So by the time Jack and I reached the finish line, together we had the makin's of two complete average humans. But they'd robbed so many parts out of my kit to build Jack, he was really one and a half humans and I was made out of what was left.

Seeing us side by side, it's easy to understand the kit theory of creation. Sort of like comparing the king of the jungle, a magnificent lion, with a hyena-anteater cross.

Oh well, I kinda like ants.

I never expected this story to generate such incendiary mail, e- or otherwise. It was as if I had trampled something sacred. In my defense, it was an innocent observation, as in "Look, the emperor is buck nekkid!"

CAVE PAINTING

So there I was, taking a snapshot of my brother-in-law. He was standing in front of drawings on a cave wall. The cave was isolated, well hidden, inaccessible, and not known to many twenty-first-century travelers.

We had been told the paintings were thought to be centuries old. It was easy in this lonesome place for me to imagine a band of nomadic Native Americans living or at least summering in this high mountain condo.

The wall motif showed humans hunting a variety of hooved, ring-tailed, and horned beasts across the rocky face. I appreciated the sanctity of what I was witnessing, but a question kept burbling up in my mind like indigestion. Why were early painters of western art such bad artists?

The warriors' hands looked like branches on a Charlie Brown Christmas tree. Their feet resembled those on a camera tripod. The elk, deer, or moose looked like sawhorses with mangled TV antennae for antlers. What I assumed to be bears could easily have been armadillos, abandoned tires, old disk blades, a carpet remnant, or elephant spoor on a Tanganyika airstrip.

It was puzzling to me. I have a second-grader. He draws people with hands. Granted, they look like potholder gloves, but they resemble hands much more than the ones in the cave painting do.

I have observed that in every group of thirty or forty people (however many a clan is), there are a few who have a natural ability to carry a tune, some who can shoot straight, some who are good with dogs, and some who can draw.

Were there no cave painters who knew which way legs bent, who could depict the shape of a buffalo, a foot, or an antler? Was it because they were forced to use the tar-and-broken-limb medium? Were they limited by the size of the canvas? Was the lighting always bad?

It has been pointed out that drawing is an art that must be refined. Realistic depiction must be learned. I guess that must be true, though it still seems to me you could raise Frederic Remington or Norman Rockwell in the wilderness, give them a piece of charcoal, stand 'em in front of a cave wall, and get a more accurate representation. Shouldn't there be some inherent ability?

The real truth is probably more shabby. The chief's daughter always fancied herself an artist, but all she could draw were stick figures. The chief decreed that no one should draw better than she, and it stuck. So the real native artists turned to turquoise, silver, and beadwork, and waited for Charlie Russell to come along and paint them realistically.

Or is this something an art history major would know?

DAVEHOLL

I have logged jillions of miles on airplanes in pursuit of entertaining the agricultural masses (I give humorous speeches for a living). I put myself in the care of those professionals in the cockpit. And to their credit, I have made an equal number of takeoffs and landings.

SPRINGTIME FLYING

I've had occasion to fly in lots of small planes. They don't bother me. I always put my faith in the pilots and let 'em do their job.

However, over the years I've developed some caution when I fly over the western plains in springtime, especially if I'm under 35,000 feet. They have some monumental weather in that swath of country, from Amarillo north up through the Dakotas. Tornado season, ya know.

One bright spring morning several years ago, I boarded a little six-seater in Chadron, Nebraska, on a milk run headed for Denver. I was the only passenger and I took the backseat. On boarding, I noticed the pilots' luggage in the compartment behind my seat. One bag was open. They set my hangin' bag on the floor behind their stuff.

I strapped in, and took out a book. The pilots were young men. They gave me the brief safety instructions, and off we went, headed south.

As we leveled out, I could not help but notice the giant wall of black clouds to my right. They rose farther than I could point. The flight was bouncy. The copilot kept checking on me. Suddenly a vertical clearing of sunlight split the storm clouds. The plane banked into the clearing. They were going to try for the scheduled landing in Alliance.

From the cockpit dashboard, pencils and sunglasses flew my way. The pilots' giant black book of maps of every airport in the world broke open and filled the air. Over my shoulder I could hear the bags bangin' around. . . . T-shirts, Fruit of the Looms, and a Stephen King novel issued from the luggage compartment. A lone dirty sock snagged on the seat back in front of me.

The pilot made a left and we popped back out of the turbulence.

Once the plane was under control, the copilot leaned back and asked about my health. "We're going to bypass Alliance," he said, "and Sidney doesn't look good either." He was the color of Cream of Wheat.

I looked back to the east. I could see all the way to Philadelphia.

"North Platte's right over there," I said, pointing.

We landed in North Platte in 52 mph winds. That's where I spent the night.

Jerry said one spring he caught a ride from Valentine, Nebraska, to Winner, South Dakota, with an Irish engineer named Joe. It was Joe's airplane. The weather was springtime rough, and Joe's plane didn't give Jerry much confidence.

When he climbed in the four-seater, he noticed Joe was wearing a parachute. "You got another one?" Jerry asked.

Joe said, "Don't worry, you prob'ly won't need one."

And speaking of airplanes . . .

CHAMPAGNE FLIGHT

Steve and Penny, good seedstock breeders from Iowa, made a trip to Hawaii to check out the thriving cattle business in our fiftieth state.

Through an oversight (she says he forgot; he says it involved the International House of Pancakes, Slobodan Milosevic, and the air traffic controllers' handbook), they were forced to purchase first-class round-trip airline tickets. They had to take their youngest out of college to pay for the trip.

They spent several days observing the big ranches on the island of Hawaii, loading feeder cattle on ships for U.S. and Canadian destinations, and making new friends.

Upon boarding for the return flight, they and the other passengers watched a Very Important Person and his entourage create a scene. He was a mid-forties hawkish-looking man with slicked-back hair pulled into a ponytail off his balding forehead. Dark eyes, gold earring, cream suit, black collarless shirt, and a diamond ring big as a dinner roll led some to think he was either a drug kingpin or a maître d' at Caesars Palace. Steve thought he had seen him at the sale barn in Winterset, but he wasn't sure.

This VIP insisted on boarding first. He bustled about his seating area, 1D—first seat on the aisle on the starboard side. He had also purchased the adjoining window seat upon which he laid his lizard skin briefcase, tungsten alloy featherweight laptop, gold lamé cell phone, and compact sound system. While all were boarding, his six vassals loaded in coach. He held up the departure to complete an important call. The entire first-class section heard him say, "Paint it robin's egg blue."

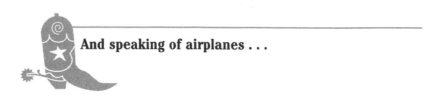

Once they were en route, his behavior was demanding, arrogant, and snotty. The passengers around him felt sorry for the flight attendant who took the brunt of his abuse. She managed to get the surrounding passengers accommodated cheerfully between the VIP's outbursts and complaints about the turbulence, bitter coffee, mediocre champagne, cheap silverware, thin blankets, and monotonous view.

Meanwhile, Steve and Penny had been rat-holing the plastic forks, unused napkins, and extra packages of nondairy creamer. The flight attendant also presented them with a bottle of champagne she had unwired but never opened. ("I'll put it in the overhead storage up front. You can pick it up when you leave.")

"The captain has lighted the seat belt warning for landing. Please remain in your seats." The plane descended from 35,000 feet into the Los Angeles airport. At precisely 1,100 feet above the runway, a gurgling, fizzing gusher poured from directly above the VIP. A Niagara of champagne sluiced from the overhead compartment along the leading edge, cascading over his hairdo, down his neck, and onto his seat.

He was screaming, trying to cover his head and unbuckle his seat belt. The flight attendant leaped to his side. She held him firmly beneath the foaming waterfall, insisting repeatedly, "You must remain seated for your own safety."

He spluttered and squinted as she did her duty. Only once did Penny see her smile, but fellow travelers were observed in various displays of mirth, from covered-mouth giggling to Steve's braying like a mule and pounding the back of his seat.

As they were debouching, the flight attendant apologized to Steve and Penny about their bottle of champagne. "The change in pressure must have popped the cork," she explained, suppressing a guffaw.

"Actually," said Steve, "we're not big champagne drinkers anyway. I'm glad you found another use for it."

Some customs cry out for further elaboration. After all, the hubcap began as a lug nut cover.

THE BUTTERFLY WEDDING

A new phenomenon is upon us . . . the butterfly wedding.

Butterfly breeders offer boxes of monarch butterflies to brides and mothers of brides. They arrive chilled and are warmed up for the big moment, then released in a golden cloud. It is very romantic and fairly expensive.

For those on a smaller budget, the moth wedding might be more appropriate.

This wedding takes place in the dark with the bride wearing a coal miner's helmet. The reheated moths are released, and the bride switches on her headlamp. For an extra ten dollars, the helmet can be fitted with a bug zapper, so the light show can be augmented with sound effects.

As this wedding fad begins to spread, I can see entrepreneurs reaching out beyond the traditional butterfly-kissin'-cake ceremony.

Imagine those sturdy folk all around the Great Lakes marrying off their daughters in a fish wedding.

It could take place in knee-deep water on the edge of a cranberry bog. Or in a hockey arena down on the ice: Choreographed just as the groom says, "I do," the entire audience in the hockey rink grandstand would repeat, "Ya, he does," and throw a six-pound mullet over the glass barrier.

The wedding party would be up to their halibut in seafood. The bride could toss a can of tuna to the expectant bridesmaids, and the best man would be clad in a rented tux and snorkel.

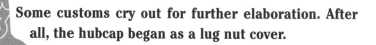

Not to be outdone, the Society for Fun with Fungus would offer toadstool weddings. The bride and groom could exchange ringworm, and truffles would be served at the reception. The wedding cake would have lichens on the north side.

It's not that those weddings haven't been done. I can remember reading about motorcycle weddings, skydiving weddings, scuba weddings, cowboy weddings, and spelunker weddings, for example. All flamboyant, planned by the couples primarily to get their picture in the paper.

But the butterfly wedding strikes me as a little less ostentatious. Beautiful but not garish.

Yet even the butterfly nuptials might be too showy for some. They could opt for a quieter theme, such as the elegant pollen wedding, the classic cheese wedding, or a subdued ceremony featuring dental floss.

Although there's no guarantee, you can never tell about some of those wild dental hygienists.

Most of the dances I've been to, I was playin' in the band. But dancin' with my wife, Cindy Lou, is one of my life's greater joys.

LAKE VALLEY

A friend of mine said, "Happiness is a honky-tonk parking lot full of Texas license plates!" I've got to say, I know what she means. They say people from Montana will use any excuse to have a party! I can vouch fer that, but Texans are right up there with 'em! What you've got to remember in Texas, though, is everybody dances in a circle. It's like a skating rink. It's easy to get the hang of it once you've learned to do the two-step.

I grew up dancin' in New Mexico. They dance the same as Texans. The first Saturday of every month, they'd have a dance at Lake Valley. Lake Valley was a ghost town ninety miles from home. The ranchers and their wives would put on the dance. It was always packed! They would start at nine, and they held it in the old schoolhouse. Ol' man Doolittle played the fiddle and stayed up by the blackboard. Anybody that wanted to could "set in" with him.

The old board floors would give under your feet, and it was always a little dusty. Little girls would dance with each other if the little boys were out of reach. Grandpas would dance with daughters, and proud young bucks would dance with their mothers or sweethearts. It was grand!

They did the waltz, two-step, polka, schottische, varsouvienne, and probably others I can't remember. At midnight we'd all stop and eat sandwiches, potato salad, pie, cake, or whatever the ladies had brought. Then the hardiest of the celebrants would dance till 3:00 A.M.

They didn't allow firewater inside, so those with a mind to would make an occasional trip to the pickup. I remember those clear nights, the silvery stars, the high sounds of "Maiden's Prayer" sailin' on the breeze, and happy people's laughter comin' through the open window of that ol' schoolhouse.

I notice in my travelin' that they're still playin' some of the same songs ol' man Doolittle played. Most honky-tonk bands will slip in "Faded Love," "San Antonio Rose," or "Double Eagle" somewhere before the night's over.

By the way, if you wanna polka—I mean *really* polka!—get up there somewhere between Glendive, Montana, and Winner, South Dakota. They really get my feet to tappin'.

I guess, when you think about it, music is good for your soul.

“Bachin’” (as in *bachelor*) on a cow camp requires the occasional trip to town to do chores, i.e., buyin’ groceries, tobacco, and parts, gettin’ the mail, and doin’ the laundry. It should be routine.

DOIN’ THE LAUNDRY

Some days it doesn’t pay to do the laundry. C.D. and Howard were stayin’ out at the ranch and had built up a pretty good pile of dirty clothes. C.D. loaded it all in the pickup, weighed it down with the toolbox, and took off for town.

A month of start-and-stop drivin’ around the ranch had resulted in carbon buildup in his diesel, so he took the opportunity on a long stretch of gravel to blow it out. He had it up to seventy and was watchin’ blue smoke and gravel spread out behind him like the rooster tail on a speedboat.

Just then a gust of wind blew his hat off. He reached over to retrieve it off the right-hand floorboard. When he looked up, the road was swervin’ out from under him as it curved to meet the highway blacktop. He bounced over the bar ditch out into the sagebrush, still in control. It was then that Lady Luck pulled the tablecloth out from under his dirty dish. He hit a concrete culvert . . . head on. It stopped him like a tree trunk stops an arrow!

The steering wheel broke off in his hand, and the pickup stood on its nose. Wrenches, sockets, hammers, socks, pliers, shirts, underwear, screwdrivers, Levi’s, and a Handyman jack catapulted over his head, ricocheting off rocks and cactus for two hundred yards down range. The pickup teetered upright, then plopped back down on its belly. C.D. staggered out and started pickin’ hankies and T-shirts off the brush and diggin’ tools outta the dirt.

Suddenly, a shot whizzed by his ear, tearing a hole in the only overshoe he’d found. He looked over his shoulder to see his vehicle . . . burning! Another shot came from the flaming unit. It was then C.D. remembered the full box of .243 cartridges under the seat. He ran for the cover of a little arroyo. As the shooting continued like the Fourth of July, he poked his head up to survey the scene. Between himself and the melting truck, which was now sending billows of black smoke as far as Wagon Mound, were tattered pieces of dirty clothes draped on the native flora, like toilet paper in the neighbor's tree.

An out-of-state car came down the highway and slowed. They peered out the window. C.D. stood up from behind his camouflage and waved a pair of jockey shorts. He shouted, "Help!" Unfortunately it was drowned out by the last .243 shell that exploded simultaneously.

The tourists calmly turned their heads, rolled up the windows, and drove on, no doubt unimpressed by their first alien cowboy sighting.

Winter can be tough on ranchers and farmers. They get up early anyway and have a lot of time to kill before the sun comes up. So, they get on the phone and bother people: feed salesmen, ag loan officers, county agents, neighbors, and, of course, their vet.

RANCHERS AND BUZZARDS

In the wintertime, ranchers and buzzards get up before daylight, put on the coffee, and wait for somethin' to go wrong. One of the highlights of bein' a cow country veterinarian is the predawn phone calls.

"DOC?"

my body is on autopilot. all nonessential functions are shut down. my brain feels like a heat-and-serve bag of frozen vegetables. the phone is cold on my ear.

"DOC, IS THAT YOU?"

witty retorts race through my mind: no, you have reached a nuclear submarine off the coast of Denmark.

"DOC, I BEEN THINKIN' . . ."

quick, call ripley's!

"REMEMBER THAT COW . . ."

certainly. i'm intimately acquainted with every one of my 40,000 bovine patients and can recall each one, even in this dense mental fog where my memory is now resting with a dead battery.

"THE ONE I TOLD YOU ABOUT AFTER THE STOCKMAN'S BARBECUE?"

also after 10 p.m., 11 whiskey sours, and a 30-minute cocktail conversation with mrs. holmes about her poodle's habit of scooting across the living room rug.

"SHE'S NOT ACTING RIGHT."

what? she voted republican? she didn't clean up her room? she's roosting in the trees with the guineas?

"I'VE BEEN WORRIED ABOUT HER SINCE YOU HAD TO TAKE HER CALF LAST SPRING. . . ."

right. too bad you didn't worry more the three days before you called me out to work on her.

"SHE'S FAT, BUT I NOTICED SHE'S SLOW TO TRAVEL. I KIN BARELY KICK 'ER OUT OF A WALK."

maybe she's hard of hearing, or just senile. you've never culled a cow under the legal drinkin' age.

"I WAS READING 'BOUT THIS SUPPLEMENT THEY FEED TO RACING GREYHOUNDS. SORTA HEATS UP."

course, you could dip her tail in kerosene and light it. no rabbit within 20 miles would be safe.

"WONDER IF THAT WOULD WORK ON COWS?"

if it does, i might try some myself, long about the first of fall.

"PROB'LY NOT. BUT JUST THOUGHT I'D RUN IT BY YOU. WELP, IT'S SUNUP, DOC. 'PRECIATE THE VISIT. SEE YA."

Rancher to his wife at breakfast: "I talked to Doc 'bout ol' number twelve this mornin'. We agreed there's nothing to worry about."

Vet to his wife at breakfast: "I had the craziest dream this morning. But danged if I can remember it!"

Mr. Flynt was an old cowboy, horse trader, and grand character. Frank was his friend and a horseman in his own right. I had no idea Frank was such an eloquent writer. These are his own words.

FLYNT AND FRANK

Andy and I went down to Williston, Florida, to visit a couple of characters. That is horse country, and these boys were hock deep in horse training. They were sure hospitable as indicated in the letter they sent after we left. . . .

Dear Bax,

Flynt and I can't tell you how much we enjoyed your visit. It was sure nice of y'all to take time to come visit, especially with that bad cold. Even though both kids caught it from you, so far only one has gone into pneumonia.

Flynt thought it was sure great that you castrated all of our colts while you were here. Although neither one of us had ever seen quite that much blood, at least we didn't have to wonder what happened when we found eight of them dead the next morning. Flynt got real excited once I explained to him how much money we were saving by only having to feed two head instead of ten. Not only that, but the two that survived sure look like moneymakers once we get them over the tetanus.

Me and Flynt can't thank you guys enough for letting us pick up every one of the bills down at the café. It never occurred to us to order steak for every meal. Thanks for the tip.

Remember when we were sitting in that bank president's office and you were telling how all the smart bankers out West were calling in their unstable cow notes? Well, sir, you won't believe this, but that banker thought that was such a good idea that he's doing the exact same thing here. By not having any cows to feed or interest to pay, there's no telling how much money we'll save this year.

And Baxter, I don't want you worrying about backing into the carport and knocking it down. In the first place, it's hard to stop any type of vehicle going 55 mph in reverse, and secondly, as you remember, Beverly only had that one big gash over her eye when we lifted the roof off of her.

Flynt was just commenting the other day about how time sure did get away from us while you were here. All of a sudden we looked up and six weeks and five days had just whizzed by. We were sure sorry to see you go, but since our livestock was about depleted and a good portion of our standing structures leveled, I guess it was as good a time as any. Oh, by the way, the folks from the car rental place came by and picked up the Lincoln and were kind enough to set us up on a monthly payment plan until the $6,300 in mileage and damages were paid off.

As Always,
Flynt and Frank

Presentation is half the meal, which is good 'cause I can't cook.

BEANS À LA BLACK—A RECIPE FOR TROUBLE

Speak to me of the humble bean,
Of Milagro, of Jack and the stalk.
Whose bold contribution has earned them a place
In the footnote of history's crock.

Recognized by poets, painters, bards, and
the literary glitterati such as Shakespeare, who said,
"A bean by any other name would still . . ."

If a bean were consumed in the forest and no one
heard it, would it still make a sound?

One small bean for man, one giant bean burrito
for mankind. —ARMSTRONG

Gold, frankincense, and pinto beans.

I never met a bean I didn't like. —LYNDON BEANS JOHNSON

A fool and his bean are soon parted. —ANONYMOUS

Quoth the raven, "Refried beans." —POE

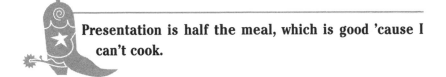

Hell hath no fury like a bean turned bad. —CONGREVE

Down through the ages, the humble bean has been treated as the blue-collar worker of the menu. The landscape on the plate, the flannel sheets for the plump weenie to lay its head. Always there, usually unnoticed like rice in China, cows in westerns, and duplicity in Congress. It has assumed the supporting role, never asking to carry the ball, ride Trigger, get the girl, or have a speaking part. Deferring always to the filet, fajita, or French onion soup.

And, even though it is a famous food in its own right, it is a frijole fame . . . like owning the most expensive Ford Escort.

Thus, to rectify this culinary snobbery, I offer my recipe for Beans à la Black:

1. Purchase ½ pound dried pinto beans.
2. Select 22 blemish-free beans.
3. Boil till soft; discard one bean over left shoulder.
4. With needle and thread, string them like beads, interspersing with capers, raspberries, and pearl onions.
5. Garnish with chili powder and lime juice.
6. Tie the fondue necklace loosely around the throat of a loved one, allowing the center bean to dangle in the angle of Louis.
7. Dine, then relax and enjoy the postprandial 21-bean salute.

At the cocktail party, a person approaches the local M.D. and says, "I've got this pain. . . ." The veterinary equivalent is "I've got this horse [dog, cow, marmoset or . . . pain]. . . ."

FREE ADVICE

There is a strange phenomenon called Alternative Faith Advice Awareness, which I just made up but can be described as this basic rule of life: Free advice is better than advice you have to pay for.

Most people have a kind of natural resentment against people tellin' 'em what to do. It hurts even more when they get in the position of havin' to pay someone to tell 'em what to do!

It's not like buyin' groceries or garden rakes, where you pay your money and walk away with something in your hand. But when you buy advice, it's a little harder to figger what it's worth. Most "professional advice," of course, is expensive.

High up on the list of professional advisers is the honorable lawyer. With the law, the common folks seem to be playin' in a game where nobody knows the rules except the lawyers. So we discuss our legal problems with those people we really trust. Like, if you had an uncle who spent a little stretch in the county jail, you'd have a natural tendency to take his advice about the intricacies of the law. Him bein' experienced and all. Only in desperation would you ask a lawyer and then you'd question his advice.

Now, if your neighbor is pretty handy and did all the wiring in the new room in his house before the fire, you'd see if you couldn't get him to help you convert the 110 in the pump house to 220. Call an electrician contractor? You're kidding!

When your cow won't get up, your pig is covered with spots, and all the hair is fallin' off the dog, who do you call? First, you call your wife's uncle. He used to raise a few hogs before he moved into town fifteen years ago. You could check his advice against that of the feed salesman and the horseshoer. Of course, there's old Dick who used to work for a vet and was pretty good at hittin' veins. He worked at the track for a while and is full of advice.

When the chips are finally down and the vet's out to the barn doin' a C-section on the old milk cow, you show him that spot on the back of your neck. The doctor in town gave you some medicine to rub on it, but Grandma says it needs a mustard poultice. Your brother-in-law offered to lance it, and you just don't know what to do. You sure value the vet's opinion 'cause everybody knows they really know as much about that sort of thing as M.D.'s. That's so, ain't it?

There's just somethin' that goes against our grain 'bout payin' for advice. I'm no different. After all, the way I keep up on the latest medical developments is by subscribin' to the *Reader's Digest.*

Even tolerant, kindhearted souls finally realize there is a point beyond which advantage of them should not be taken. Good for them.

DRAWING A LINE IN THE DIRT

Sometimes you've just got to draw a line in the dirt. Tolerance of bad behavior should only go so far. Like Sam, who, when asked to judge a Texas chili cook-off, disqualified a contestant from Milwaukee whose recipe called for noodles. "You've got to make a stand," he said. "Goulash is good but it's not chili."

Jerry is a kindhearted musician. He often receives invitations to come and perform, many from friends who say, "We can't pay you anything, but it will be good for your career." One day, Jerry realized, Wait a minute . . . this is my career! He drew a line and doubled his income.

There are many hardworking parents who send their kids to college. Their children profess interest in meaningful fields of study like marine biology (tern cleaner), world peace coordination, or compassionate preschool psychotherapy. Tuition increases, bills mount, majors change, yet graduation remains a distant star.

Till finally one day, the twenty-five-year-old student finds he has been volunteered for the UN Peacekeeping Force stationed in Two Dot, Montana. A diploma is not required.

Then there were the two cowboys who threw paint on the protesters in front of the fur store.

Or the team of masked raiders who washed Don Imus's, Howard Stern's, and Chris Rock's mouths out with soap.

Or the patient folklorist who responded to the question "I write cowboy poetry; can I tell you one?" by saying, "No, thank you. If you do I will fill your hat full of mashed potatoes and pull it down over your head so far, french fries will be coming out your . . . ears!"

How 'bout folks that sit down next to you, whip out their cell phone, dial, and say, "I'm at the airport," and you can hear the caller on the other end say, "So what?" You can just be thankful they're not calling you, or you could whip out a bottle of rudeness repellent and douse them down.

I was at the rodeo recently and saw a lady take matters into her own hands. She was sitting behind a cowboy wearing a big hat. She tapped him on the shoulder and said, "Young man, I cannot see around yer hat. Would you mind removing it." He explained how it was improper for a cowboy to remove his hat at a rodeo except for the national anthem.

But she had made her point, so I just traded places with her.

Ah, the confidence of youth.

HOLLER TAIL

There she lay. Uncomfortable but chewing her cud. She hadn't gotten up for a couple days. "Milk fever," I confidently diagnosed to myself. Treated simply, and often miraculously, with intravenous calcium.

Uncle Leonard looked over at me, his nephew who had finally made it into veterinary college. "Whattaya think it is, Bax?"

"I suspect it is a case of hypocalcemia caused by a depletion of calcium as a direct result of recent heavy lactation," I replied knowledgeably.

He looked at me like you'd look at a feebleminded dog who had just messed on the carpet.

"It's holler tail, son."

"Hollow tail?"

"Yup. Treat it with salt and ashes." With that, he went to the house and returned with a bowl of furnace ashes and a Morton Salt box. He cut a gash on the underside of the cow's tail with his pocketknife. The cow's expression went from total boredom to immediate interest.

He sprinkled a few ashes in the incision. The cow cocked an ear. Then Uncle Leonard put a handful of salt in the wound and massaged it briskly. Bossie's eyes popped open like she'd backed into the fender of a '58 Cadillac!

The cow rose and staggered across the pasture.

Uncle Leonard did it all as calmly as a mother leopard teaches her clumsy, big-footed kittens how to kill a gazelle and eat its liver.

My feeble excuses faded on my lips. I stopped short of suggesting that had I bent *him* over the kitchen table, buffed his buns with an electric sander, and liberally sprinkled him with

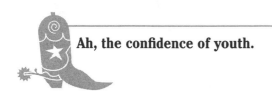

Lawry's Seasoned Salt, he, too, might make an astonishing recovery.

The horror stories of young, mistake-prone veterinarians are legion. Mine are no different. Animals I had pronounced dead or beyond help lived for years afterward to haunt my practice. Others in obviously good health, the ones I scolded the owner for even calling me about, died before I got the bill made out.

I guess I should have known it wasn't going to be easy my first day on the job. I walked into the vet shack on the feedlot. The cowboys were drinking coffee, warmin' up. I had on my brand-new covies. They had a big *V* on the pocket, and thermometers and doodads hung all over my body.

"I'm the new veterinarian, gentlemen. I expect we'll have no problems getting along. I'll teach you as best I can and be glad to answer any questions concerning veterinary medicine you should have. I look forward to working with you for the betterment of the cattle, the crew, and the company."

It was quiet as hair fallin' on an army blanket.

Eventually, crusty ol' Bud got up and walked by me to the door. He turned, and said, "Kid, I was punchin' cows 'fore you could drag a halter chain."

Then, followed single file by the other tight-lipped cowboys, they left me standing in my glory.

VET
SALT
© 2001

SPARKLING CONVERSATION

In daily conversation, do you often find yourself groping for just the right phrase? Yer listener hangs politely, mouth agape in wild anticipation of some profound description. You say, "Yessir! That rain we got yesterday was as welcome as . . . welcome as . . ." After a long pause, you finish the sentence with that moldy old expression ". . . the flowers in May!" Wow!

Wouldn't you feel better if you had thought of "welcome as the ace of spades in a hand of lo-ball poker!" or "welcome as nine yards of gravel in a muddy driveway!" We have developed several standard descriptions for "dumb as . . ."; "nervous as . . ."; "cold as . . ."; "sleepin' like a . . ."; "happy as . . ."; and "crazy as. . . ." We can all fill in the blanks with assorted posts, churchgoers, well diggers, babies, clams, and loons. But if you really want to be known as a scintillating conversationalist, you need to come up with some phrases that are a little more offbeat:

"Hot as a seat cover on a Phoenix Fourth of July!"
"Flat as an armadillo on a Texas highway!"
"Nervous as Jell-O on a vibratin' bed!"
"It was so cold, I saw two coyotes tryin' to start a jackrabbit with jumper cables!"
"It was so hot, I saw a dog chasin' a cat and they were both walkin'!"
"It was so dry down home, we had to pin on our postage stamps!"
"Popular as a pink Cadillac salesman at a Mary Kay convention!"
"Safe as a side of bacon at a bar mitzvah!"

"Happy as a cattlefeeder with an optimistic broker!"
"Handy as a zipper on a banana!"

Sometimes descriptive phrases can have a less than flattering connotation:

"Handy as a pocket in yer underwear!"
One of my employers said that havin' me help was like havin' two good men . . . not show up!
"Cute as a cancer-eye cow!"
"He worships the people she walks on!"
"The committee had all the wisdom and insight of a band of Suffolk bucks!"
"Tasty as hair in the gravy!"
When two unlikable people find each other and get married, it only demonstrates that "one good dog deserves another!"
"He needs another car like a tumbleweed needs a telephone, like a frog needs an earring, or like a cowboy needs a checking account!"

These meetings are a regular part of life in the agricultural community. It is a way of presenting the latest innovations in animal health or crop production to the ranchers and farmers—producers, if you will. I have personally participated in many before I became a former large animal veterinarian.

THE PRODUCER MEETING

When you take a seat in the waiting room of a veterinary clinic, a feedlot office, or an animal health store, you occasionally notice people sitting there who look out of place. They are often dressed in a more formal attire than most clientele. They may be doing their "times" ("two times two is four, two times four is eight, etc. . . ."); they may be reading the ten-year-old copies of *Look* magazine; or they could be annoying *you* . . . just killing time.

These dedicated individuals, who seem to take precedence over no one in the animal health food chain, are company reps. Salesmen armed to the teeth with research trials that support their product, special offers to entice volume buying out of season, and lunch money. They are the mainstays of our continuing education.

They seem to exude a certain tension, which is understandable: They have the job security of a smoke jumper.

A big part of their regular duties is producer meetings. Some of these meetings go well. Others . . . well, others prove that masochism builds character.

John works for an international pharmaceutical company that offers products for use in livestock. He arranged with the manager of a good-sized feedlot to put on a meeting for the cowboys and vet crew employed therein.

A local steak house was selected as an appropriate location

for the meeting. Supper and drinks were furnished as bait. A good crowd of eighteen or twenty showed up for the meeting.

No separate room was available, but the maître d' had set up a single long table that ran the length of the room, wall to wall down the center of the dining area. John set his movie screen against the back wall at the end of the table. The slide projector sat in the middle of the table between the two rows of attentive cowboys.

John began his presentation. He started with lung diseases. Pictures of fulminating pleuritis glared from the screen, attracting the attention of random diners. Presently, an incidental customer walked between the projector and screen, excusing himself politely as his shadow darted across a rather explicit slide of chronic suppurative pneumonia. As John was soon to discover, he lay in the direct and only path to the rest rooms.

The wayfarer returned, tripping over the projector cord, which gave everyone a moment's respite from pulmonary contagion.

Just as John segued into injection site abscesses, he was interrupted by the waitress, who stepped into the spotlight, and asked, "Who ordered the scotch and water?"

Then, in the midst of his discussion on rumen physiology, a group from the other side of the room broke into song. It was "Happy Anniversary to You," dedicated to a couple celebrating fifty-eight years of wedded bliss: "Happy anniversary . . ." ". . . methane . . ." ". . . to yo-o-o-o-u-u-u. . . ." ". . . is released along with . . ." "Yeah, yeah, applause. . . ." "Scuse me, I gotta go to the john. . . ." "Sure, . . . carbon dioxide. Any questions?" "Yes, who ordered the two whiskey sours and the Bud Light?"

On the drive home, John commented to his boss, "All in all, it wasn't too bad a meeting."

"Yeah," the boss said, "but ya know, they might've missed some of the details."

I spent my life living where the work was. Now I live in a community that my wife and I chose. It's kinda nice.

MY KINDA TOWN

How to describe my kinda town . . .

1. It has no restaurant called Le Sans Souci.
2. The local environmentalists are both ranchers.
3. You give your phone number by using only the last four digits.
4. Gas is at least ten cents higher than that in the nearest town with a Wal-Mart.
5. The paper comes out once a week, and high school students sit at the post office and sell it on Wednesday mornings.
6. You can see clear out of town both directions from the one stoplight.
7. Soccer (T-ball, girls' basketball, etc.) moms control the social activities of the community.
8. The local radio station operates at fifty watts, covers five square miles, and has a real disc jockey.
9. The feed store, the barber shop, and the coffee shop act as the disseminators of early breaking local news.
10. You are noticed and missed when you don't make it to church.
11. The mayor and city officials control the real estate in town, but they are kept in line by local watchdogs who contribute a steady stream of letters to the editor regarding fishy political activities.

12. Both video stores are closed on Sunday.
13. The grand marshal for the fabulous Butterfield Days Parade can shoe a horse and weld.
14. One-stop shopping is available at the Vitamins—Furniture & Gospel store.
15. The FFA is bigger than the football team.
16. Everyone has at least one neighbor who is a member of the volunteer fire department.
17. Kindergarten through twelfth grade are all at the same school.
18. You can still get two scoops of ice cream for $1.50, credit at the lumber store, and a tractor tire fixed.
19. On the official city seal is a cow, a locomotive, and a box of dynamite.
20. And in my kinda town, people are just as busy, just as smart, and just as good-hearted as folks who live in towns big enough to have a restaurant called Le Sans Souci.

According to my calculations, my town would have to triple in size before Wal-Mart would consider building here. We're safe for a while.

SMALLVILLE GROWING PAINS

Letter to editor of Smallville paper:

". . . Smallville needs more food stores, drug and hardware stores. How come only Safeway is in Smallville? No competition. Smallville doesn't change. Gas prices stay high. The few stores that are there charge too high of prices. They don't care. That is why we shop in Metropolis, sixty miles away. At least there is competition. When will the people of Smallville ever learn? Sir, when my subscription runs out, no more renewals."

L.D., Smallville

Therein lies the dilemma of Smallville, and Smallvilles all across the country.

If we were to ask Mr. L.D. why he lives in Smallville, he might answer, "Less pollution, less crime, no traffic jams, local school control, better view, more peaceful atmosphere, friendlier people, . . . it's easier to be a big fish."

Supply and demand is a basic rule of economics. It is also safe to say that big-time supermarkets, hardware stores, discount warehouses, movie theaters, fast-food chains, and pharmacies have studied and are aware of every Smallville from sea to shining sea. Their research staffs know to the nearest gnat's eyebrow the population base and buying power of each community. And when the time is right they *will* strike. And when they do, they will replace and eliminate those businesses presently supplying the needs of Smallville folks. To the point that they are the only places in town to shop. Then they will raise their prices until demand stimulates even bigger competition. On and on and on.

The only way to please Mr. L.D. is for Smallville to become more like Metropolis. To grow until he himself becomes an anonymous fish in a crowded sea of goods and services. Then he will begin complaining about the congestion, the crime, the pollution, the long lines, and the fact that no one listens to him anymore.

So he will move to another Smallville where life is at a slower pace, he can still get served coffee by a real waitress, have a charge account at the hardware store, where the barber knows his name, and the local paper will print his letters to the editor.

For those of us who live in Smallville, there's a little Mr. L.D. in each of us. We should be careful what we wish for.

In the cowboy world, there is a stigma to wrangling dudes. It's the equivalent of professional wrestlers in athletics or psychiatrists in the medical community. "Glamour jobs" in a world of hoof and horn.

COMING OUT

There are few things more painful to watch than the "coming out" of a cowboy.

I had known Don for twenty-five years. Known his family, sat at his table, and leaned on him now and then. He was a good ranch manager in his day. He did things the cowboy way and was honest as a cedar post.

I recently ran into him and we had a warm reunion. "Whatcha doin' now?" I asked. He sort of hemmed and hawed. "Oh, I been doin' a little day work for a fellow up the road."

"On a ranch?" I asked.

"Not exactly . . ."

"A feedyard deal?"

"Well, no . . ."

"Let me guess," I harassed him. "Yer leadin' tourists around the desert on a bunch of ol' plugs and tellin' em what a great cowboy you were?" I laughed at my joke. He turned pale. I suddenly got embarrassed. "I was only kiddin'; I know you wouldn't ever . . ." His eyes began to well with tears.

"You mean . . . ?" I asked. He nodded mournfully. "I'm wranglin' dudes. . . ." I glanced around nervously, not wanting any of our cowboy friends to overhear.

"I just sort of fell into it," he snuffled, and began to confess. I handed him my hanky. "We moved to town where my wife could get a good job. I tried selling western clothes, building saddles, even tried to be a movie extra, which is awful close to wranglin' dudes, then finally this carny–kiddie ride guy offered me a job tendin' his dude string. The grandkids were back with us, we needed the money."

"It's not so bad," I said, patting his shoulder. "You'll get back with the cows sometime."

"No . . . I'm already a marked man. I've learned some yodeling tricks. They tip bigger if you tuck yer pants in yer boot tops and wear a stampede string. I've even started writing cowboy poetry. I go by the name Sagebrush."

"Surely not!" I put my arm around him. It was an emotional moment. "Yes," he said through the tears, "I even have names for the horses—Fury, Black Beauty, My Little Pony, Buttermilk. . . ."

I stopped him. "They have clinics, ya know. There's one in Luverne, Minnesota. Not a tourist for miles. You can get back to basics. Saddle, rope, cow."

"It's no use," he said, catching his breath and sighing, "It's just that . . . I like it. They think I'm king of the cowboys! They like my stories. I'm a hero like John Wayne or Billy Crystal or Robert Redford . . ."

"Why they couldn't even pack your saddle," I snorted.

"I know," he said, "but we're all in show business."

I shook my head sadly. "Sorry ol' pal. Well, I'll see ya. I gotta go make some promo spots for my next appearance at the big western Art Fest and Boot and Spur Show."

***Therio,* from the Greek *therion,* meaning "beast," and *geno-,* from the Greek *gennan,* meaning "to produce." As opposed to genuflect, *Genyplasty,* an operation for restoring the cheek, or gentoo, which is a penguin abundant in the Falkland Islands.**

THERIOGENOLOGIST

Theriogenologist? I was one and didn't even know it! A specialist in animal reproduction. An ovary observer, a diddler of the zygote. One who devotes his life to preserving pregnancy . . . a cow plumber.

Included in this broad field would be embryo transplanters, diagnostic palpaters, infertility detectives, fertility evaluators, artificial inseminators, and others identified by their green fingernails and white socks.

Those folks who practice this profession are an unusual group. They don't wear a tie to work. They approach their business like a professional football player, knowing when the game's over they're gonna look a lot worse. It is not a career for the fastidious.

Dick Butkus or Burt Reynolds would have been good theriogenologists. However, I can't see Fred Astaire or Michael Jackson at ease in a pair of muddy five-buckle overshoes, with manure in their ear. They would make better equine practitioners.

People who work at the rear end of a cow develop a similar personality. They're usually "good ol' boy" types who have a high humiliation level. If one were easily embarrassed, under a cow's tail—"behind the gun," so to speak—is not the place to be.

There are dangers. Like the veterinarian who was preg checking one fine afternoon when the cow went down in the chute, breaking his arm. The fractured bone pierced his plastic sleeve and lodged him securely inside the cow like a fishhook.

But most injuries are more damaging to one's self-esteem. Gary was a struggling newlywed who was doing artificial insemination to supplant his meager graduate student income. He arrived at the dairy with one plastic sleeve in his kit. It lasted for five cows. Gritting his teeth, he approached cow number six and palpated her barehanded. Gruesome, perhaps, to the non-cowperson, but an acceptable alternative to the dedicated theriogenologist. As he began his treasure hunt in the final cow, he must have said something "unprofessional" because she kicked him on the inside of the thigh. He was elbow deep in holstein at the time. She clamped down on his arm as he fell to the ground writhing in pain.

Driving home that evening in stinking agony, he made a terrifying discovery. He had lost his untarnished, twenty-four-karat, diamond-studded, five-year-payment-plan, once-in-a lifetime-extravagance, two-month-old wedding ring . . . inside the cow!

Next morning, he returned to the dairy, armed with a metal detector, and was seen for days wandering through the fields, going from patty to patty like a beachcomber high on propane fumes.

The bride was not happy. The mother-in-law was vindicated, however, since she had warned her daughter not to marry someone who makes a living that no one can pronounce.

People would understand a lot more about life if they could think like an animal. It's called anthropomorphism, attributing animal traits to humans.

CAT LAWS

I was reading the paper to the cat last week. She tries to keep up on current events, particularly stories about Ivana Trump and alien landings. We got to a story where a few obscure animal rights groups were calling for the nation's 66 million pet cats to be kept indoors for life.

"Why?" asked Miss Kitty.

"Well," I answered, "this says that free-roaming cats kill from 8 million to 217 million birds a year in Wisconsin alone."

"My, I had no idea there were that many birds in Wisconsin."

"Yes, and one person was quoted as saying, 'We don't want our house companions going out and killing other animals.' "

"What about mice?" asked Miss Kitty, scratching behind her ear.

"They don't say, but they are also worried about you being eaten by coyotes."

"Then why don't they keep all the coyotes indoors for life? It's like making people bolt and bar their homes and stay inside during prime shopping hours. Why don't they just keep all the criminals indoors for life?"

"Good question, but they say cats are domesticated animals and coyotes are wild animals, and they don't want to appear anti-wildlife."

"Mice are wildlife, so are birds; it's all part of the food chain."

"They apparently want to remove cats from the food chain. For your own protection, of course."

"I thought it was to protect the birds," said Miss Kitty, ever vigilant to flaws in my logic. *"And besides, do they really enjoy that odoriferous cat box in the laundry room? It's bad enough to walk*

Wisconsin OR BUST
WISCONSIN BIRD PRESERVES
QUAIL O' THE SEA
FLAKE LIGHT
TUNA
BOB BLACK '01

around in a Tupperware toilet if you're a cat. I've always envied camels. Sand as far as you can see. Go anytime you please."

"They suggested that humans who want their cats to spend time outdoors need to invest in an outdoor enclosure, or walk their cats on a harness."

Miss Kitty got indignant. *"You ever tried to walk a cat in a harness! We're not dogs, you know! I've spent a lifetime keepin' your place free of rodents and vermin, and this is the thanks I get. So I eat a bird now and then. And another thing, I've lost more friends to car tires than coyotes. Why don't they have speed limits slow enough to let cats get out of the way."*

"Wait a minute," I protested. "It isn't me; it's just a story in the paper."

"Sure," she huffed, *"but some self-appointed cat lover will weasel or badger you into makin' me a house cat. You'll fall for it and take me prisoner. Next thing I know, you'll be takin' me for walks in a cat harness. Not for me, buckaroo. I'm leavin'."*

"Wait," I pleaded, "Where will you go?"

"Well," she said, *"I've always wanted to see Wisconsin."*

I've always had a fascination with marketing and admire the warped and neurotic minds of ad agencies' geniuses. They cast their seeds to the winds hoping for a fertile field or at least a crack in the sidewalk in which their idea can take root. It is more an affliction than a profession.

CHICK-FIL-A

There is no doubt that the dairymen have had a runaway success with their "Got Milk?" and milk moustache advertising campaigns. But the latest promotion idea that's caught my eye is Chick-fil-A.

It's a fast-food chain specializing in chicken sandwiches. The pitchman . . . or woman . . . or bovine, actually, is a holstein cow. They feature eye-catching billboards with lifelike cows climbing the sign graffitiing it with messages like "Eat more chicken. All in favor say, 'Moo!' "

I've always sort of enjoyed the internecine competition between edible species.

Beef, because it is the priciest and most distinguished of the products, is usually the object of the slings and arrows of the other, no less nutritious but less prestigious commodities. Beef's advertising reflects the almost military approach to its promotion. Big, solid, no nonsense. Even the most remembered beef ad, Wendy's "Where's the Beef?", was a little heavy-handed.

Pork has a lock on sausage, bacon, and barbecued ribs—fare produced by an industry that can laugh at itself a little because it has no serious competition. But then they tried to move in on chicken's "Light and Lean" territory by claiming to be the "Other White Meat." Unfortunately, they are saddled with a name that conjures up images of oversize linebackers gnawing ham hocks. Think how much easier it would be to sell pork had it been called swan or ocelot or dolphin. I can't even think of a single vehicle named after pork to enhance its image. We've got Dodge Rams, but no Buick Boars, Pontiac Pigs, or Saturn Sows. So pork is stuck with its succulence as its best-selling feature.

Turkey, too, has got the same "name" problem. It should have been named something befitting its exalted position on our holiday tables: "I'm going to slice the Suava Royal. Who would like white meat?"

An unfortunate, difficult-to-market name has kept many other commodities from becoming regular American table fare: anteaters, for instance, chiggers, and Saint-John's-wort.

But chicken started at the bottom and has pulled itself to top as the most consumed meat in the United States. The industry hasn't depended on scintillating advertising. They don't worry that the name of their product has synonyms like *cowardly, scrawny, pimpled, or fowl.* They just have a good, cheap, nutritious product that tastes like whatever you put on it.

And now they have enlisted cows to help sell Chick-fil-A. The ultimate indignity. Next thing you know, they'll have celebrity cows with a mouthful of feathers and egg on their face, saying, "Got Chicken?"

CHICKEN HOUSE ATTACK

The competition between the beef and poultry industries has become a full-time marketing theme, but rarely has it become as personal as the "Whitefield Chicken House Attack," aka the "Battle of the Bramer and the Broiler."

It was a hot summer afternoon in Haskell County, Oklahoma. The foggers and cooling fans were going full blast in Jim's twin five-hundred-foot-long chicken houses. "A wet chicken won't die" is the motto of *polloqueros* down south.

Sniffin' around the ten-foot-tall screen door at the south end of a chicken house was one of Jim's seven-hundred-pound black Bramer-cross steers. Nibblin' on the rice hull and litter, he pushed through the door, and it slapped shut behind him.

"Blackie" froze for an instant. He found himself in this high, long metal building filled with more suspended, humping, fizzing, spritzing, undulating, augering, grinding, whirring water pipes, feed lines, sprinkler heads, fans, braces, cables, hoses, and attending racket than the engine rooms of the *Monitor* and the *Merrimac* . . . not to mention the combined uproar of 25,000 startled chickens!

Blackie panicked, bore to the right, and headed down the east wall, leaping, smashing, and obliterating the watering and cooling system that hung below the three-foot level. Racing for the big door on the north end, he careened along, bending the galvanized automated five-hundred-foot-long feed line into a mangled horseshoe. Jim, astride his four-wheeler, had seen the steer enter. He was racing alongside the building watching the mayhem through the five-hundred-foot-long chicken wire–covered side window.

He screeched to a stop at the north door to open it and let Blackie escape . . . bad plan. Blackie saw him, turned back, and tried to jump out the side window. The long span of chicken wire allowed him to actually exit the building but sprang him back like a trampoline into the pipes and feeders on the west side. Down the wall he went, demolishing everything in his path until he stopped midbarn to consider.

Jim four-wheeled it back to the south side door, propped it open, and strode into the melee. Blackie pawed the ground. Feathers fluttered and litter flew. He charged. Jim, thinking quickly, reached down and armed himself with two stomped-flat chicken carcasses. Grasping their feet, he wielded them like a sword and a mace. Much noise ensued as hair and feathers flew, but Jim prevailed and Blackie hightailed into a brush pile a hundred feet away.

Jim looked over his shoulder, back into the *Titanic.* There they were—24,998 chickens pecking through the wreckage as if nothing had happened. He looked back to the brush pile. Blackie glared, shook his head, and snorted fluff like a busted pillowcase. And though Blackie never came near the chicken house again, Jim said he could track him in the woods for days. He'd swallowed so many feathers that his cow pies nestled in the grass like big doilies on the back of Grandma's lime-green sofa.

Machinery and cowboys . . . oil and water.

A CLOSE CALL

Talk about takin' a beating . . .

I stood on the porch at Dale's horse farm and soaked up the view. It was deep springtime in west Tennessee. The grass was so green, it hurt your eyes. The dogwoods were in bloom, and two sleek and shiny horses grazed in the picture. It looked like a cover off the *Quarter Horse Journal.*

"Nice fence," I said, commenting on the pole fence circling Dale's pasture.

"Thanks," said Dale, "but we had a heckuva scare buildin' it. See that post? . . ." I noted a stout post at the end of the driveway. The harrowing tale unfolded.

Dale had decided to build this fence last spring and finally got around to it in December. He enlisted the aid of two friends, Chuck and Phil. They all dressed warmly since it was twenty degrees the day they started.

At the particular post in question, the boys were havin' trouble diggin' the hole. It was close to the paved road, and the ground was hard.

Dale backed his tractor up to the future hole and poised the posthole auger over the designated spot like an ovipositing wasp. The auger spun on the surface of the frozen ground.

Chuck, who's big as a skinned mule, pulled down on the gearbox. No luck, Chuck. So Phil stepped between the auger and the tractor and leaned his weight on the horizontal arm supporting the auger.

Now, Phil had come prepared to work in the cold. He had on his hat with Elmer Fudd earflaps, mud boots, socks, undies, long johns, jeans, undershirt, wool shirt, and Carhartts.

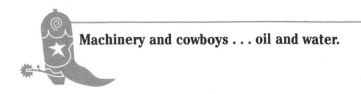

Carhartts, for you tropical cowboys, are insulated coveralls made out of canvas and tough as a nylon tutu.

Phil gave Dale the go-ahead. Dale engaged the power take-off. The auger clanked and started to turn. Suddenly Phil seemed to explode in front of Dale's eyes!

Dale engaged the clutch immediately, and everything stopped. Phil stood before them naked.

I said naked. Not quite. He had on his boots and his belt, still snug through the belt loops. The jeans had been ripped off his body from the pockets down, leaving only a small piece containing the fly. It flapped like Geronimo's loincloth.

Dale's explanation for his friend's near denuding was that Phil's pant leg had brushed up against the extended arm of the PTO. In a split second, as fast as Superman could skin a grapefruit, the PTO had torn all the clothes off Phil's body. In less than three minutes, his body turned blue. Nothing was broken, but he was as bruised as the top avocado at the supermarket. Chuck commented later that he looked like he'd been run through a hay conditioner.

I figger he was the blazing example of that expression "He looked like he'd been drug through a knothole."

NATURE'S LOGIC

I was marveling at my horses' tails as they stood around in the shade. A perfect fly-shooing machine.

Then I wondered . . . if it's so perfect, why doesn't a cow have a tail like a horse? The answer was obvious. A cow pie is usually much looser, more liquid than a road apple. If a cow had a horse's tail, it would always be a stiff and sticky mess, unless a cow could preen and lick itself like a cat, which of course it can't.

It's the same difference between people with moustaches and people without them. Evolution has predestined that the hair lip will be more prone to personal grooming. You may have noticed mustached cowboys constantly fondling and striking their facial hair. Just survival of the fittest.

This continuing analogy applies to women's feet and frequency of marriages. Observation: In the last forty years, the size of the average woman's foot has grown two sizes. Women's fashions used to lean toward sleek, pointed footwear. A graceful extension of the curvaceous calf, delicate ankle, and dainty foot.

Then women's feet began to grow. Attempts to gird a size 11, triple A, in a bullet-shaped shoe led observers to imagine giraffes in giant elf shoes or Admiral Peary cross-country skiing the Arctic wasteland.

And the number of marriages per person has increased considerably in conjunction with increase in foot size. Obviously a direct result of the female of the species being easier to track.

But back to the horse's tail. Its simplicity of design and utility of function has inspired many copycats in nature. Teenage girls wear their hair back in a ponytail and coordinate their swishing with gum-popping.

Not to mention the German shepherd, kite flying, or the landing parachute on the tail of a Russian bomber.

And every spring we see the ultimate adaptation of that equine appendage. Millions of new graduates standing in robes facing their futures, eyes glazed, palms sweating, and yet virtually fly-free thanks to the tassel. Wave on, eohippus. We are forever indebted.

My youngest was born when I was forty-eight. I tell people having a child at this age just makes the time crawl by.

UNCLE BUCKER'S BABY

I saw Uncle Bucker the other day. He's not really my uncle; that's just what everybody calls him.

"So," I said, "Uncle Bucker, I heard the news. Congratulations! A boy, huh!"

"Yes," he said, "and at my advanced age, you can be assured that it wasn't planned!"

"Bucker," says I, "yer not much over fifty, are ya?"

"Naw, but it was sure a surprise. Miss Mattie suspected something, I guess. She went to the doctor, completely unbeknownst to me. When she came back, I was standin' there in the livin' room, mindin' my own business.

"She marched in from the garage and stopped on the edge of the carpet. Close enough that I could see that look. You know the one. It's the same one she uses on the dog when he messes on the carpet. She quickly explained that the rabbit had died. And I didn't even know he was suffering!

"It was such a shock that I lapsed back into my ol' livestock training and began to babble, 'Well, yer, uh, bred . . . uh, you'll begin to notice some changes in your body as the gestation progresses; your skin will get smoother and you might . . . bag up a little.' 'Wait,' she says, 'Doctor Hamstra told me that no matter what you say, it's not like a cow!'

"So they shamed me into the breathing lessons. Let me tell you, son, you young pups may not realize it, but there was a time when expectant fathers engendered respect. There was a special room on the delivery floor for expectant fathers. It had Barcaloungers, ESPN, and a wet bar. When the nurse burst in with the good news, you'd stand up and pass out cigars to all your fellow new fathers. You can't even light a cigar in the parking lot at the hospital today!

"Then you'd rush down the hall, duck in, and kiss the new mother and kiss the new baby and go directly . . . to the bar . . . where you could be with people who could appreciate your contribution. You weren't just another face in the delivery room on the second row, trying to shoot the video over the crowd.

"So, like I said, they shamed me into the breathing lessons. I think they helped a little. My only real memory of the delivery room was the doctor looking up from the barrel of the cannon, so to speak, and asking, 'Would you like to cut the cord?'

"I was doubled over a folding chair in the corner, practicing my breathing, when Miss Mattie, who had other things on her mind, said, 'No he doesn't!'

"But I'm doin' better now that he's a little older. I was worried for a while. Looked like he was gonna be a farmer."

"Really?" I said.

"Yep. Till he was six months old, all he did was milk and scatter manure!"

Squabbling amongst Christian religions is the equivalent of sibling rivalry. Sometimes it gets bitter. It makes parents, even those on high, exasperated.

MORMON BOYS

That they would find each other would have been as unlikely to predict as the fall of communism or the good sheep market. She was old and a lifelong Southern Baptist. They were young and on a mission for the Mormon Church.

A requirement of good "Mormonism" for young men is to serve as missionaries for the church for two years. They are expected to go door to door wherever they are sent and spread the gospel of the Latter Day Saints (LDS), also called Mormons.

Now if you think that's easy, put yourself in their place. You are nineteen years old, most likely from a rural background, have no car, and are in a strange place. You're also wearing a dark suit and tie, riding a bicycle, and knocking on strangers' doors. As you know, many who open those doors and find out you are "peddling religion" are not friendly.

They knocked on her door one day and explained their purpose. She said, "Well, I'm teachin' our home Bible class." They excused themselves and left. Later she said to her husband, "I'll never turn those boys away again."

Eventually they came back down her street, and she said what she says to everybody who's ever knocked on her door: "Have ya eaten yet?" Well, for two boys a thousand miles from home and batchin', nothin' sounded sweeter.

For the next eight or ten years, the Mormon boys "stationed" in her little Oklahoma town beat a steady path to her door. They overlapped each other every few months, and each new missionary was taken to meet Uncle Leonard and Aunt Effie.

Many of these boys were country raised and homesick, I'm sure. They are not allowed to call home except on Mother's Day. Effie and Leonard were retired farmers, both in their eighties, and sure knew how to cook for hungry boys. The boys played Skip Bo, ate fried chicken and peach cobbler, helped Effie with her garden when Leonard became unable, sang while she played on the piano, and found an oasis from the pressure.

Uncle Leonard passed away last fall, and Effie's havin' health problems. I visited her in the hospital recently, and she talked about her *Mormon boys.* Her face lit up. It was obvious how much they meant to her. Some still write, and the new ones still come by checkin' on her.

I'm sure they discussed religion, but as Aunt Effie told 'em, "Yer out walkin' the streets for your Jesus, He's my Jesus, too, and that's more than most religious folks do. I'm proud of you."

She saw their need and filled it the only way she knew how. She offered them kindness. And if you ever questioned that passage "It is more blessed to give than receive," you ought to see her face when she talks about her *Mormon boys.*

I don't know if they're better Mormons or she's a better Baptist for their knowin' one another. And I don't know if the leaders of the Southern Baptist Convention and the Elders of the church of the Latter Day Saints would approve. But I do know that the human race is a little better species because these two folks took the time to appreciate one another as people.

I received a letter written in Spencerian script from an older lady who chastised me for presenting subjects in my commentary she said were not discussed in proper mixed company. She had grown up on a ranch, and in her family it was not allowed. She concluded by scolding me and saying, "I guess things have changed." I wrote back and respectfully said, "Yes ma'am, they have."

TALKIN' DIRTY

In my commentaries I have often mentioned scours, manure, abscesses, big tits, bad bags, cancer eyes, foot rot, slurry pits, afterbirth, retained placenta, castration, heat cycles, sheep pellets, and snotty noses.

Over the years, I have received the occasional letter castigating me for talkin' dirty.

It is never my intention to offend the sensibilities of my readers. My poems and stories are always written with the idea that people who read them regularly are livestock people. In real life, I'm not comfortable cussing or telling blue stories in mixed company.

So, if I'm talkin' to a cattlewoman, I assume she knows what bull semen is. That she has had scourin' calves in her house and knows what it means when someone says it's rainin' like a cow peein' on a flat rock. Those subjects are part of her lifestyle. I feel no need to ask her to leave if I'm doing a rectal exam on a cow.

Farm kids are the best example. They are what we have taught them and what they have experienced. Fifteen-year-olds who are learning to artificially inseminate learn the proper words for the anatomy involved. *Uterus* has never been a dirty word to them.

Children on a dairy farm learn to spot cows that are in heat.

Washing the bag or tit dip does not send them into fits of teenage giggling.

Helping a newborn get his first meal is not a titillating experience. Mucking out the horse barn is hard work, but it's not "ooky"!

All of us who spend our lives tending livestock are aware that our daily working vocabulary is not always proper amongst people from outside the real world (gentiles, I call them). When our new preacher, who hails from Chicago, is introduced to us, we don't immediately invite him to the oyster fry next Tuesday.

I would guess the people who are most conscious of this "cowboy vocabulary" are new spouses marrying into a livestock-raising family. I'll bet they could write a book!

So, to those of you sensitive folks who read my commentaries with some reservations, or have neighbors who sit at your dinner table and talk about how to get cow manure stains out of a good shirt, I beg your indulgence. It's not dirty to us, it's just grass and water.

Just about the time I get to thinking my dog is almost lovable, I catch him mouthing a road apple or draggin' a piece of javelina haunch home. Maybe decorum is not something I should expect in a cowdog.

DOG ROLLIN'

There are some deep philosophical questions that cry out for explanation: Is there really life after death? Do fish ever get tired of seafood? And why do dogs roll in fresh horse manure?

To the dog's credit, it doesn't have to be horse's manure, and it doesn't have to be fresh. It can be old garbage, big-game offal, varmint remains, unrecognizable roadkill, swamp water, sewage drains, rotting cabbage, putrifying hen eggs, cow pies . . . virtually anything that would make a maggot nauseous.

For three weeks, my next-to-worthless all-American cowdog, Boller, came home smellin' like fish. And friends, it didn't waft off him with the delicate aroma of fresh trout frying in lemon and butter. It was like opening an apartment door on a dead buffalo in August.

I gave him several baths and kept him chained at night. All to no avail. Finally I cut him loose and tracked him across the road. Our creek had run full early in the spring, then went down. It had stranded some Boone and Crockett carp on the bank. Boller went over and played with them every day. Left his new rawhide bone on the porch.

I quizzed him about his filthy habits. He looked at me with that same exasperated expression I had seen on my uncle Dink when I asked him why he drank warm buttermilk.

I considered and discarded the theory that it is some instinctive protective device. Can you imagine a pack of wolves trying to sneak up on a herd of caribou after rolling through a pile of whale droppings and dosing themselves liberally with polar bear vomit? The caribou would pick 'em up as soon as they cleared Canadian customs!

It occurred to me it might be an insect repellent. Certainly it would offend the discriminating bug, but I doubt if that includes ticks, skeeters, flies, lice, bedbugs, fleas, or your average bloodsucking bat.

Maybe it has something to do with making them attractive to a prospective mate? There are certainly some modern corollaries in the human race that lend credence to this theory. A whole industry is based on making us smell like Pine Sol, cheddar cheese, or a rutting beaver.

Even if I could figger out the reason for this revolting animal behavior, I doubt it would make Boller any easier to be around. I do know this: Be careful letting a dog lick your face, for the same reason you should hesitate before shakin' a veterinarian's hand. . . . You never know where it's been!

BONNIE AND DAN

Bonnie and Dan are a happy couple. Jack was merely a ship in the night. Bonnie is a bullterrier. Best described as a forty-pound blunt Cheeto with stubby appendages and a pointy tail. Maybe more like a twelve-inch concrete pipe with an antenna.

Roughhousing with her is like playing with a cinder block. Why anyone would own something designed to "tarry bulls" could be explained by applying the same logic to Porsche owners: Why would anyone own a car that seats two, costs more than a B-1 bomber, looks like a Jerusalem cricket, and goes 140 mph? Companionship. Bonnie has tight skin, a breed characteristic she shares with bankers, so that her eyes have an oriental look and she always appears to be smiling, which she is! She is affectionate by nature and the perfect companion for Dan, a retired curmudgeon who still curmudges part-time.

Enter Jack. Bullterrier with a pocketful of genes . . . bullterrier genes, chromosomes to be more precise, in sizes X and Y, which he deposited on her uterine doorstep.

Bonnie became great with puppy . . . and delivered the single offspring to great expectation. Alas, tragedy intervened, and the anticipated heir to Dan's affection did not survive. Dan was stoic, Jack was indifferent, but Bonnie was distraught.

The day after delivering, Bonnie was found burrowed in a dark corner of an old wooden ammunition box. For two days, she lay in the box, leaving only to tend to necessities. Finally Dan peeked into her hiding place with a flashlight, and lo and behold, there lay his missing slipper. He had made it himself out of elk hide, leather thongs, and braided rawhide buttons. It was wet and wadded.

Bonnie came rushing back, nearly knocking him over, and lay down next to the slipper. She licked it lovingly and nudged it with her nose toward her swollen breakfast nook. For the next four days, she nurtured and protected the nest. Any time

Jack would approach, she'd come bursting out of the box, snarling like a mama grizzly.

Dan gave her the time and space she needed to get over the loss. Although, he did ask around about when to wean slippers. By the time she recovered, his handmade elk hide footwear looked like a hippopotamus cud.

Well, another season has passed. Bonnie is great with puppy again. Dan is thrilled and Jack is indifferent. But deep in her heart, I suspect Bonnie is hoping that the new baby will look as much like Dan as the last one.

MARGINAL QUOTES

- "As long as you've got good elimination, you've got it made."—Uncle Leonard
- "If a man can't drive in a bar ditch, he's got no business on the highway."—Tink
- "When asked how she got to be president, Anita replied, 'I missed the meeting.' "
- "You can't use too much tape."—Dr. Allen
- Tom H. says, "I enjoy all company. Some when they arrive, some when they leave."
- "A true friend will tell you if yer hat's on backwards."—Calvin
- "I'd rather be at the head of the ditch with a shovel than at the bottom with a decree."—Tom on irrigation rights
- "If they won't come, you can't stop 'em."—Yogi B.
- "He's stooping to new heights."—Sandy
- "His eyes are so squinty, they could blindfold him with dental floss."—Buck
- "They teach chickens to lay eggs by walkin' back and forth in front of them with a hatchet, humming, 'Mmm, mmm, good, mmm, mmm, good. . . .' "—Doug
- "The right to be heard does not include the right to be taken seriously."—Hubert H.
- "If you wanna put out a fire, start yer own!"—Hoot
- "Cowboys walk in parts."—Peter
- "You have to know Mr. Dewey well in order to dislike him."—Margaret T.
- "Looks like his bad luck has peaked."—baxter
- "Horseshoein's not so hard. It's just the dread of doing it."—Carl

- "His sleeping bag smelled like they drove geese into it and beat them to death."—Oly K.
- "It's been a month of Mondays!"—Sheryl
- "I don't deserve this award, but I've got sinuses and I don't deserve them, either."—Ace R.
- "Sometimes you have no choice, so take it!"—baxter
- "If yer smart, you'll always believe in Santa Claus." —Judy
- "Sure you can sell out when things are good. But then what will you do?"—John
- "Of course your waffle is tough; you ate the potholder."—baxter

When one of my cowboy friends tells me he's getting married, my first question is "Does she have a job?" This particular wedding took place in the pines of Arizona. I thought that I would never again see such a group of ill-prepared misfits as these groomsmen. Then President Clinton appointed his cabinet. But whatever magic took place, it must have worked; they're still married and she's still got a job.

COWBOY WEDDING

There's two things a cowboy's afraid of: Bein' stranded afoot and a decent woman. I went to a cowboy wedding recently where the bridegroom had found him a decent woman. This was not yer normal walk-down-the-aisle, kiss-the-bride kind of wedding. This was the merger of two Arizona ranching families, complete with rings made outta barbwire, a fiddle playin' "Here Comes the Bride," and mosquitoes.

The families had worked for weeks gettin' everything ready. Three days before the main event, they set a big tent up in the meadow for the reception and dance. Up came a big storm and blew down the tent. They said when it blew down, it looked like a fat lady sittin' on a roll-away bed.

The bridesmaids all looked beautiful in their long dresses. The groomsmen, however, presented a different picture. Putting a suit coat on some of those cowboys was like puttin' croutons on a cow pie. The sisters had made them all gray suit coats and bandannas. Weddings seem to make cowboys uncomfortable. These fellers looked like they were still hanging in the closet—paralyzed!

Part of their condition could be attributed to the forty-eight-hour bachelor party that preceded the knot tyin'! The groom was maneuvered around on the wedding day like a NASA moonwalker. Sleep had not been allowed, and, with the bride's permission, his blood alcohol level was just below Extremely Flammable.

The appointed hour arrived. The priest got up and explained that this was not a normal Catholic wedding (he was wearing a sport shirt and jogging shoes), but it would be legal just the same. Everybody, and there was a bunch of them, got seated in this pretty little cove, complete with a lagoon in the background. It was like God had made this spot just for the wedding.

It rained a little but no one cared. The bride was lovely. She stood out like a penguin in an asphalt parking lot. The priest asked Dad, "Who gives this woman in matrimony?" He replied, "Her mother and I and the Valley Bank." When it came time for the kiss to seal the vows, the bride and groom spit out their chew and laid to it.

At the bride's request, we played "Walkin' the Dog" as the wedding party marched out. It was fitting, I guess, 'cause Billy's ol' dog, Bronc, caught the bouquet.

Seems there's a lot of mileage gotten by lamenting the cowboy as a vanishing breed. But if you don't live out here with the cows and the brush, how would you know? It would be like me writing odes to the vanishing cricket player. I don't see any or know any, so they must be vanishing. Let me assure you, though some may have a job in town, there are still plenty of cowboys out there who can get the job done.

REAL THING

He was lookin' for work. I was buildin' corrals, stretchin' wire, layin' rock, and clearin' brush. I asked him what he could do. He said, "I'm a cowboy." For six months, Frank built corrals, stretched wire, laid rock, and cleared brush. He worked hard and stayed on. It was skilled labor but hard on the back and hands.

Last spring, I went to Gerald's branding and asked him if I could bring along an extra hand. Gerald said the more, the merrier. "Can he ride?" he asked.

"Well," I replied, "he told me he was a cowboy."

We got to the ranch and Gerald got him mounted. Frank had brought an old rope but no chaps or spurs. We rode out to gather the bunch. Gerald asked me if I'd drag calves to the fire, since we were shorthanded. Flattered, I said, "You bet." By midmorning, we'd gathered a hundred or so cows with calves into a tight trap.

On Gerald's orders, we were trying to sort out a big high-horned half-Bramer barren cow. Four times we got her to the gate, and four times she broke back. Gerald was determined, and he *is* a good cowboy. He roped her and started draggin' her toward the gate. She went down. Wouldn't budge. Stuck like a D-8 Cat in a cranberry bog.

"Git another rope on her!" Gerald hollered. While I was

fumblin' around tryin' to unleash my rope, I saw a beautiful flat loop sail over my horse's nose from left to right and settle around the cow's butt. Frank's rope came tight. One hard pull, and she was on her feet, then Gerald and Frank drug her out the gate. The dynamics of our little group changed perceptively.

Thirty minutes later, we had 'em in the branding corral. All but one two-hundred-pound black bally calf. He was wild as a deer, and it took us several tries to get him back up to the fence, but he couldn't find the gate. Gerald eased up to within ten feet, threw an easy loop, . . . and missed. The calf spun like an Olympic swimmer and shot between us. I heard a whiz and a whoosh. Frank had thrown his rope from a sideways position, fired it like a harpoon, and caught that calf goin' straight away on a dead run at twenty feet.

Gerald looked at me. "I b'lieve I'll ask Frank if he'll drag 'em to the fire."

"It would be the right thing," I said, with a newfound respect we both felt. Frank, whose real name is Francisco, is still buildin' fences and settin' posts for me. There's lots of Franks and Franciscos and Bobbys, Josés, Eddies, and Rogers out there sellin' feed, teachin' school, drivin' trucks, and pickin' strawberries. Drawin' a paycheck.

That's what they do, but it's not what they are. If you ask 'em, they'll look you straight in the eye and tell ya, *"Soy un vaquero."* . . . "I'm a cowboy."

DAVE HOLL

THE COWBOY IMAGE

The livestock business has an effective symbol that has withstood the loving treatment of Hollywood, Nashville, and Madison Avenue. It is the cowboy.

Hollywood made heroes of cowboys who always got the bad guy, practiced safe shooting, and could leap on their horses from a burning train! Then John Travolta gave us the urban cowboy who could disco, and wore a straw hat made of oatmeal, rattlesnake heads, and sweepings off a chicken house floor!

Nashville turned us into four-wheel-drive cowboys. Yodelers with pompadours who drank too much and looked like a cross between Roy Rogers and a Filipino bus!

Madison Avenue has given us chain-smokers and colognes called Stetson and Chaps (as in, that sure "chaps" my butt!), all designed for men who don't wear socks!

Through it all, the public's image of cowboys has remained positive. The anti–livestock industry groups have had a tough time tarnishing our symbol. It's been hard for them to portray the American cowboy as a money-grubbing, animal-abusing land raper. They whack away at it persistently, often using the ruse that the cowboy is a vanishing breed. That he no longer exists, and therefore, this symbol that everybody loves has no connection with the modern livestock business. This myth continues to be promoted to the point that we are often asked, sadly, if it is true our way of life is dying.

To this, I reply no. Of course not! Who do you think is takin' care of the cows? But, they say, we never see them.

There is a good explanation why you never see cowboys. It is possible to get in a car and drive from Philadelphia to Fresno and be completely insulated from the territory you cross.

The car is climate controlled. You never roll down the windows. You pull onto a freeway that is the same from one end of the country to the other. Although you drive through green to brown from high to low, you never have to change the cruise control.

You come down an off-ramp into virtually the same self-service gas station/convenience store. You use the same credit card and buy the same cardboard coffee and irradiated snack cake.

You turn on the radio and hear a trained generic disc jockey playing the same canned tape of Top 40 hits. You stay in the same temperature-controlled Holiday Inn or Motel 6, see the same CNN or HBO. You eat at the same Denny's or McDonald's.

It is possible to drive from one end of the country to the other in your enclosed gas-powered cocoon and never smell air or touch dirt.

However, on either side of the road, even in what appears to be desolate country, you can find homes, schools, roads, farms, and ranching communities thriving. And cowboys. Lots of 'em! The only thing is, friends, you just can't see 'em from the road!

The idle mind will come up with something, anything, to keep from takin' an 8 to 5 job.

KEEPIN' BUSY

"Skip, whattya doin' nowadays?"

"Oh, I'm doin' a little day work for Irsik and ridin' two green colts for fifty dollars a month. I think I've just about sold that load of salvage lumber I traded Mr. Jolly out of.

"Some guy came by the other day and wants me to audition for the Marlboro Man. Said they pay pretty good even if they don't pick me!

"I've put the down on some green pasture. If my pardner comes through, we're gonna turn out a few steers.

"I've got some other deals workin', playin' guitar with Butch and Jim on Fridays at the Fort, shoein' the odd horse now and then. Ol' Man Gammon pays me to irrigate his yard every other Sunday.

"Other than that, . . . not much."

Thank goodness his wife has a job! Skip is one of those fine fellers who eases through life from one project to another just fillin' in the gaps.

He's the man you can call at noon on Tuesday and get some help. Chances are he could hook up a trailer and go pick up something for you at the sale. 'Specially if you gassed him up first!

He's one of the few individuals who never misses a ropin', a weekday grade school track meet, a car wreck, a beer bust, horse sale, pancake feed, or political rally.

He'd no more think of makin' a "career change" that would require his movin' outta town than he'd consider filing his income taxes on time!

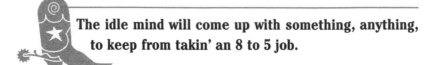

He was offered a seasonal job with the highway department as a sign fluctuater but declined at the last minute 'cause somethin' came up.

I've always been curious what he writes on a form when it asks his occupation. Executive Enabler? Implementation Specialist? Relationship Analyst? Impediment Counselor? Maybe just Omniconsultant.

Everytime I visit with him, the list of what he's doin' changes. A few items come off the top of the roll; some new ones are included at the bottom. But he's always gotta lotta irons in the fire.

He's the inspiration for that ol' Coyote Cowboy proverb "If it takes somebody more than ten minutes to tell you what they do for a livin', they're probably self-unemployed!"

There's lots of us cowboys who've spent our lives workin' for the absentee ranch owner. They put clothes on our backs, feed our families, and let us do what we do best: take care of the livestock and the land. Like bosses anywhere, there's good ones and there's bad ones and some are a little eccentric.

STRONG WORDS

Some words are to be tasted, others to be swallowed, and some few to be chewed and digested.
—Francis Bacon, 1561–1626

"What's the new owner like?" I asked Roger.

"When he replaced the forty-year-old plumbing in the company house, he went to the top of our list. Plus, he understands cows and is learning the ranch. But he's a hard charger. He'll be flyin' down this afternoon."

For the visit Roger had borrowed from the local car dealer a brand-new Ford four-wheel-drive, three-seater Excursion with big tires, rhinoceros paint, and a bad attitude. When John, the tycoon, arrived with Larry, his sidekick, we all four loaded into the Excursion for a tour of the ranch. The winter snows had been heavy in northeastern New Mexico. The vast meadows and juniper covered peaks were picturesque. The snow had melted and the ground was soaked. The ranch roads were seriously muddy, and we put the Excursion to the test. Soon the side windows were partially obscured and the windshield speckled. John seemed to enjoy each pitch and yaw.

When the smell of hot antifreeze seeped into the cockpit, I thought maybe John would suggest we turn back, but my experience with entreprenurial giants, CEOs, and middle linebackers is . . . they *never* turn back! John was sort of a cross between Sir Edmund Hillary and Evil Knievel, maybe even a civilized Ted Turner, or like a Lexus with a front-end loader bucket.

On we went across the ranch, whiplashing back and forth and fighting for the high ground. Roger was clinging to the wheel like Captain Ahab, and John was exhorting him to stay the course. Larry debouched to open a gate, and we locked through like a towboat on the Mississippi. Our post-banging fishtail trowled a layer of mud up Larry's front. When he turned sideways, he looked like an eclipse.

We clawed to the top of the next hump and saw the county road.

"Whew," we exhaled.

"We have a flat," exhaled Roger.

The right front tire, big as a 757 jet intake, was flat on the bottom. Less than six inches of clearance showed between the axle and the saturated earth. We crawled underneath and dug a hole to accommodate the eight-inch jack. In the waning thirty-two-degree sundown, we rotated the handle and watched the jack sink out of sight in the soft ground without lifting the vehicle one micron. "We need something hard and flat to put beneath the jack," proclaimed John. There were no rocks on the treeless plain. "How strong are your words?" he asked me.

I thought he was referring to my recent display of colorful language. But he pointed to the box of my books nestled in the backseat. It took three of my new 224-page, full-color, brilliantly illustrated hardback books to allow the jack to raise the three-ton Excursion high enough to apply the spare. The books sustained considerable damage. They were transformed into the shape of a Jell-O mold and received third-degree literary lacerations, though not as severe as some of the book reviews.

"Strong words," said John as I scraped baseball-sized chunks of mud off my misshapen poetic volumes. "I'm sure glad it came out in the hardback edition."

A little slice from my autobiography.

SUMMER HOME

Over the years, I have tried to give the impression in my commentaries that I am a suave, sophisticated, Cadillac cow person. Sort of a knight in a broad-brimmed hat and jingling spurs. Steeped in western lore and an ardent defender of the code of the West.

Some of you might have pictured me in my young manhood sitting on the porch of my giant ranch home, sipping a light beverage, and surveying my vast cow herd grazing to the horizon. I admit I have not done much to discourage this image.

This spring I revisited a sentimental chapter in my seedy past. As I drove up to the crumbling line shack out behind the feedyard south of Roswell, a chill ran up my spine. Stucco was peelin' off the chicken wire in big chunks. Somebody had pasted cardboard in the broken windowpanes. Rusty car bodies and assorted, dilapidated machinery were scattered amongst the weeds in the yard. The round corral was fallin' out around the top, and the bob wire sagged on the posts. As I looked at that tired ol' house, I wiped a speck of dust from my eye and thought, Somebody has really improved this dump!

Thirty years earlier, I had moved into this ghetto reject in the middle of the night. Well, not exactly "moved into" . . . more like broke-and-entered and camped. I had pried a piece of corrugated tin off one of the windows. By flashlight, I laid out my bedroll and slept, exhausted.

I discovered next mornin' that the last occupants had left in a hurry. All the furniture remained, including the sheets on the bed. There were even some canned goods in the pantry. Everywhere I walked, I left tracks like a moonwalker in the dust.

I swept it out, took the tin off the windows, and aired out

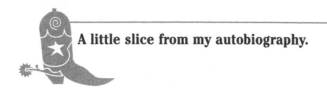

my new summer home. The fresh air seemed to drive out most of the house pets, except the scorpions. I finally just gave them their own room. There was a nest of rattlers under the kitchen porch. I battled them all summer, and they didn't get in the house, much.

Within two weeks, I had gotten the electricity turned on, but I never did have running water. I packed it from the nearest neighbor. I established a slit trench and kept a shovel by the door. The shovel was handy for killing snakes, too.

I finally located the place's owner in California. I wrote and offered to pay him rent. He wrote back and suggested thirty dollars a month. I sent him fifteen and figgered that that would cover the whole summer.

Despite my outgoing personality, I never could get any friends to stay overnight except my brother, who was as dumb and broke as I was.

I've ridden a lot of borrowed horses in my day. Sometimes they treat me kindly, other times they test my salt. I like it either way. I just like horses . . . even spare horses.

SPARE HORSE

"Come go with us, Cal," invited Lee. "It'll be a beautiful ride, and Mel's got a spare horse."

A spare horse? pondered Cal. As in extra like spare time, or thin like crow bait, or frugal as in sparing, or duplicate as in spare part, or a horse that is called in when the tenpin is left standing?

"Why not," Cal agreed. Lee also assured him they had a spare saddle. They gathered in the scenic Wasatch Mountains in the shadow of Mount Nebo. The spare horse turned out to be a good-sized bay mare. . . . "Good," thought Cal, who weighs in at 250.

However, the spare saddle that Mel brought was indeed spare. It had no back cinch, no breast collar, and a narrow fork that didn't fit the mare very well.

"I traded work for this spare saddle. Didn't cost me a dime!" bragged Mel, who was a lug tightener at Big O Tire.

Lee held the mare's lead rope tight as Cal began his ascent of the sixteen-hands mare. Left foot in the stirrup, hands on the horn, he placed his weight to spring. The saddle slipped to port. Mel stepped in to help just as Cal's right foot arced up from the ground. The heel of his right Justin roper, at roughly the speed of sound, made solid contact with the fork of Mel's family tree.

Mel barked like a dog and dropped to his knees.

The mare spooked and pulled back on the lead rope. It burned through Lee's hands, peeling an ear-sized chunk of

hide off his right palm and fingers. He wailed like a tomcat with his tail caught in the door.

The mare bolted, and Cal was left behind suspended in midair, levitating horizontally for a microsecond. One almost expected a magician to appear and run a hoop over his body to prove there were no wires.

Alas, the microsecond ended. Cal fell like a roll of wet carpet and landed flat on his back with a thud. He never bounced. The rest of the crew was too impaired from laughing to help him up. When he finally got his wind back enough to sit up, Mel was standing semi-erect and Lee was licking his palm.

"You still wanna ride?" asked Lee.

"It depends," said Cal.

"You could ride my other horse," offered Mel.

"Is it a spare horse?" asked Cal suspiciously.

"No," said Mel, contemplating his answer, "I would say it is a primary animal."

I took a course (bad pun) in golf in college but never mastered the game. I only play now when I'm forced to. They never ask me back.

GOLFING DISASTER

I played in a celebrity golf tournament in Oklahoma City a while back. Now, I've been to a few celebrity team ropings, a couple celebrity dogfights, a million brandings, and one celebrity rock pickin'—but this was my first celebrity golf tournament. Generous people paid a lot of money to play golf with well-known folks like Joe DiMaggio, Mean Joe Green, and Red Steagall. The money was donated to help the blind.

I got in the golf cart with a feller named Phil. He asked me what my handicap was. I couldn't think of anything real bad except an addiction to Miracle Whip; however, I was told at one time that my nose would qualify me for a parking space.

He asked me how well I played. I said not too well. I'm sure he thought I was bein' modest, because after the first hole he turned to me and said, "You really don't play golf too well, do ya?"

You play eighteen holes to a game. I don't know why they invented that number. You would have thought they'd play ten or a dozen or an even twenty, but for some reason they choose eighteen. Probably the first golfer just played till his arms were sore and decided that was enough.

When you get down to the nitty-gritty, there's two weapons you use in the game: the driver and the putter. First, you line yourself up between two swimming pool floats and "tee off." This is done with the driver, which is a fly rod with the handle sawed off. Only my gun-bearer and guide knew which way to aim. He'd stand up beside me and point off to the horizon. Then tell me to hit the ball off in that general direction. It was always necessary to clear spectators back 180 degrees from my line of fire. It was impossible to predict which direction my ball would go. By the third hole, we'd traded our golf cart for an all-terrain vehicle and the rest of our group was riding in an armored personnel carrier.

Once you make the green, it is recommended that one use a putter. The only comparison I can make to putting is that it's like shooting the eight ball on a table where the navy has been landing jets. I think I could drop the ball from a hovering helicopter and have a better chance of hitting the hole. Finally, they let me putt with a snow shovel. They said it improved my game.

A nice feller lent me his golf bag and a pocketful of balls. I lost six of 'em. I was ashamed to tell him. I'm sure he thinks I stole 'em. I lost so many balls that we eventually rented a backhoe for the sand traps and hired two scuba divers to join our caravan.

They haven't asked me back. But maybe I'll get invited to a celebrity bowling tournament; at least I won't lose as many balls.

In retrospect, it took a pretty strong woman (Cindy Lou) not to intervene on my behalf and explain that I was not in my right mind. Where's Hunter S. Thompson when I need him?

GETTING OUT ALIVE

It had been one of those days, and all I wanted to do was get out of town alive. I'd spent three days on horseback and got the job done without incident. Certainly nothing classed as a felony, anyway. Cindy Lou picked me up in the rental car. While loading my belongings I managed to lock the car keys in the trunk. I couldn't find my guitar and discovered I had left my airline tickets in a restaurant thirty miles away.

Doggedly I pocketknifed my way through the padded backseat to retrieve the keys. I tracked my guitar down to a lonely parking lot where it was waiting faithfully like a good dog. And I located the restaurant, after three calls, to save my tickets.

After arriving at the John Wayne Airport I decided to send a postcard to my Aunt Effie. On the way to the gift shop, I stopped at the stamp machine. Seventy-five cents, it read, for three fifteen-cent stamps. "What a deal," I thought as I pumped three quarters into the slot. I pulled the lever, and nothing happened. The coin return gave me fifty cents back. Thinking I'd made a mistake, I put seventy-five cents back in, pulled the lever, and nothing happened again. I pushed the coin return and out came two quarters—again.

"Aha!" I said to myself. "That's how this works!"

I jiggled and shook the machine vigorously. I pounded it. Finally I picked it up and turned it upside down. It weighed about eighty pounds, big as a stop sign. I was so intent on retrieving my quarters, I didn't hear the screaming. I was interrupted by a tap on the shoulder.

"Is there a problem?" asked the officer, stepping back two paces and unsnapping his holster.

Three of them escorted me through the gathering crowd. I heard the mumblings: "Lynch him!" "Get the vermin off the streets!" "See, Billy, that's what happens when you don't eat your broccoli!"

I sat quietly in the steel interrogation chair while the deputy explained that I was being "officially detained" while they ran an FBI check on me.

As he questioned me, witty retorts raced through my mind:

> "What do you think you were doing?" (Trying to weigh myself?)
>
> "Do you have some explanation?" (One small step for man, one giant leap for the postmaster.)
>
> "Are you aware that tampering with a stamp machine is a federal offense?" (What's the difference between tampering and revenge?)

All the while, Cindy Lou stood quietly thumbing through the phone book. "What were you doin?" I asked when I was later released on the condition I leave town.

"Oh, nothing really, just jotting down the number of a bail bondsman."

Mel and the Cajun Kid were top hands in the rodeo business in their youth. They can sure tell stories.

A STICKY GIFT

Mel said the Cajun Kid meant well. They had been rodeoin' together for years. So Mel knew that Kid's gift was sent with the sincerest intention. It never occurred to either of them that the lid would loosen in the mail!

Kid grew up in sout' Looziana. In his youth he helped make ribbon cane syrup on a mule-driven press. He'd fed the cane into the machine, which mashed out the juice. Dat's wot dey made dem syrup wit! Wuddn't as thick as molasses, but it sho wuz sweet!

Mel walked down to the mailbox. It was a hot summer mornin'. Not oppressive, just the pleasant birdsongs and bees a'hummin'. As he closed in on the mailbox, the hummin' got louder. Soon he could see herds of bees flyin' over like geese in winter! Beneath his feet, columns of ants marched in single file down the path. They had two infantry and one armored division!

Flies zipped in like fighter planes, butterflies drifted aloft like weather balloons, and a pod of hummingbirds whizzed around the target!

At first glance Mel thought his mailbox was a grizzly bear! The post was covered with a moving carpet of every crawling critter with a sweet tooth! The box itself was swarmed with layers of bees in the shape of a buffalo head!

He took a long stick and pried open the door. The floor was sticky with syrup. Although the can was packed in a wooden box, it was not syrup tight. Ribbon cane syrup oozed over the side and dripped toward the ground like lava. Two-, four-, six-, and eight-legged varmints stood underneath, mouths agape like baby robins!

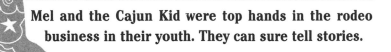

Using a branch, a piece of baler twine, and a broken chunk of sheep wire, he fished out the wooden box. It hit the ground with a *thunk* and a gurgle.

Mel ran to the house, backed the pickup down the road, and shoveled the shipping box containing the can into the bed of his truck. He mounted the seat and sped down the highway. He was followed by a black cloud that could be seen and heard two counties away! He maintained 85 mph six miles before he finally outran the last of his pursuers!

He retrieved his precious cargo, noted the return address on the box, and headed home. As he turned up the drive, he noticed, to his relief, that the plague of syrup slurping varmints were gone. So was his mailbox! The whole bunch had mobilized and just packed it off!

KIDS

I was expressing concern about my eight-year-old son, whose "talking in class" keeps him staying after school on a regular basis. In spite of discipline, threats, and punishment, he still relapses now and then. Granted, he's remorseful, but sometimes, I guess, he just can't help it.

After hearing my lament, my friend and philosopher W.C. just shrugged and said, "You can't swim outside the gene pool." It was a hard blow to swallow.

When I was in the sixth grade I had my first man teacher. He was retired Air Force and a strict disciplinarian. Demerits were given for talking or misbehaving. A monitor was appointed in each row to keep track. Staying after school was the consequence of too many demerits. Those who had a minimum were promoted each week. That way we learned about military rank. By Thanksgiving there were girls in my class who were five-star generals. I made it to corporal once.

My daughter has inherited her mother's "keep a stiff upper lip" and "get even" stubbornness. I used to take great delight in hiding behind a door or leaping out from behind the couch shouting, "BOO!" Sometimes she'd cry, but what the heck, she was just a little kid. One Saturday morning I staggered into the kitchen, groggily poured some milk on my Cheerios, and sat down at the table. It was a quiet morning, overcast, cold outside, no leaves on the trees, tan grass, gray bark, chirpless birds, "not a creature was stirring, not even a mouse." Or so I thought.

Sneaking from her second-grade, little-girl bedroom came revenge on her hands and knees. Stealthy as a Navy Seal, down the stairs, across the rug, through the kitchen, right up under the table where I sat oblivious as Pompeii the day before Vesuvius blew.

I was wallowing my spoon around in the bowl trying to spell

Oolagah, staring at the sliding door that looked like a blank movie screen, not yet able to form a coherent thought. I grasped the bowl as a primate would, to slurp. Suddenly, rising like a Trident missile, thirty-six inches from my pursed lips, across the table appeared the most terrifying visage I had ever seen. It was accompanied by a bloodcurdling scream that would break glass.

My mind could not compute. My "fight or flight" mechanism kicked in, the chair went over backwards, the table rose six inches off the ground, and the air was filled with flying objects, both edible and inedible.

I crashed!

My heart pounding, I crawled back up and peeked over the tabletop. All I saw was the back of a seven-year-old kid wearing pajamas and pigtails, swinging a stuffed rabbit. She walked back to her bedroom.

I couldn't see her face, but I think she was smiling.

Gosh, I'd of loved to be there that night with those boys. I really like that last line.

EDDIE'S BOAT RACE

Butte, Montana, is famous for many things, not the least of which was Eddie's Downtown Midnight Power Boat Race.

Eddie did day work for Randy and Leroy. That summer, he helped them refinish houses. Eddie was mostly labor but he was good at it. They paid him $250 a week, and he had to borrow money on Thursday to make it to the next payday. Eddie bought a lot of beer. At six feet and 260 pounds, he could hold a lot of beer! He hadn't had a haircut since his sister's wedding, and his beard looked like the ground side of a bale of hay.

Eddie had a change of heart one night. He decided to cut down on his party life. As therapy he chose to rebuild his boat. For three weeks, he'd go home every night and work on it. It was a seventeen-foot outboard, sleek-lookin' craft, which he had sitting on sawhorses in his front yard. He stripped and sanded, varnished and patched, rubbed and polished, and tinkered. It was beginning to take shape the night he fell off the wagon.

Leroy had his own boat up at the lake, forty miles away. About 2:00 A.M. on a balmy Friday night, Eddie suggested to Leroy they oughta take a boat ride. He was persistent.

Finally, Leroy said, "Awright, you lunatic! I'll take you for a boat ride!" But instead of goin' to the lake, he drove straight to Eddie's house. Eddie climbed in his boat. He thought it was hilarious! Leroy dropped his thirty-foot chain through the eyebolt on the prow and laced it around his trailer hitch.

"Hit it, Leroy!" yelled Eddie. He thought it was a great joke. He thought that right up until Leroy popped the clutch and jerked the boat off the sawhorses! You could see the whites of Eddie's eyes!

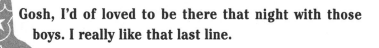

Down through the garden they went! Tomato vines, chicken wire, and stalks of corn slapping the sides! Eddie was ducking the melons and ears of corn when they wheeled onto the empty street! Rooster tails of mud flew from behind the pickup; fruit tree branches and fence stays sailed in all directions! Eddie had a death grip on the steering wheel as the boat banked and swerved. He was stiff as a hedgerow post, and his lips were frozen in the shape of an O. With his hard hat pulled down and his cutting goggles in place, he looked like a walrus in the Indy 500!

The boat careened at the end of the chain, throwing a shower of gravel off the port side! The city road crew had graded a long strip of gravel and left the extra piled down the middle of the street. By careful driving, Leroy was able to whip Eddie and his crumbling, shattered hull back and forth across the gravel hump.

Splinters, aluminum siding, fiberglass, wire, cans of paint, leaves, dirt, and rocks sprayed like tornado droppings in the wake of Eddie's speedboat! As the bottom of the boat disintegrated, it filled with gravel and ground to a stop.

Eddie stepped from the shipwreck, shaking. He asked for a Coke and said, "Tie 'er up, boys, before she sinks!"

BOB BLACK '01

I spent two months livin' in Kansas City when I was thirty-five. I'd grown up in a small town in a county that was 65 percent Spanish-speaking and was not really aware of racial divisiveness. Kansas City at that time was still healing old wounds from the race riots. When I strolled into that blues nightclub, I had no idea I was an integration pioneer. Funny what innocent ignorance can do.

WILLIE'S TOTAL EXPERIENCE LOUNGE

Prejudice is a funny thing. When a city slicker or a dude comes meanderin' into a Montana bar in Glasgow, he's liable to get a lot of hard stares. But, I'm here to tell ya, when the shoe's on the other foot, it can be mighty uncomfortable.

I set out one night in Kansas City to find one of them "down-home guitar blues pickers" that I had read about in the Sunday paper. I was drivin' around Saturday night lookin' for Walter's Crescendo Lounge. I had some ribs at Money's on Prospect and asked directions. The feller told me not to go over there after dark. Then, after thinkin' about it, he scribbled his name and phone number on a piece of paper and said, "When you git in trouble, have 'em call me." Nice of him, I thought.

Somehow I never found Walter's, but at the corner of Thirty-ninth and Jackson I spied Willie's Total Experience Lounge. I recognized the name from the paper, so I went in.

I was dressed normal: hat, jeans, and boots. The bartender was a lady named Bert. She served me a scotch and cream soda.

I sat at a table in front of the band. As the clientele came in, they all sat around by the walls. Kind of like they were circlin' me. Nobody said much and they weren't real friendly. Finally the bandleader, Freddy, came over to my table and asked me, "Hey, man, what are you doin' here?"

I told him I heard this was the best music in Kansas City and I came to find out!

Well he must have thought the same thing 'cause it sure tickled him! He couldn't do enough to make me feel at home. His sister was the waitress, and he told her to make sure my grape Nehi never went dry.

By then, I "wuz smarter'n a tree full o' owls, ten foot tall, and bulletproof!" But I couldn't get nobody to dance with me! Eventually this lady named Elizabeth consented. She must have figured I wasn't so bad after all 'cause she sat at my table and invited Louise and Wilma to join us. The four of us danced until closin' time. It was a fine evening, and although they didn't take to me at first, they must have decided that cowboys aren't from outer space, just different.

I remember that little lesson when I see a kid wearin' a headband and sandals in a cowboy bar. I always try to give 'im the benefit of the doubt. After all, he might be friskin' customers at the door next time I make it to Willie's Total Experience!

The cowboy and his dog. Tighter than two dice in a crapshooter's hand, joined at the heart and faithful as a tapeworm. Oh, to be loved like that.

COWDOGS

A good cowboy should have three things: a good horse, a good dog, and ______. I left the last one blank so you could fill in your own. Some might choose a good woman, others a good banker, a job in town, a silver bit, a full can of Copenhagen, or Saturday off.

Now, every fall when I go out to work the cows, the neighbors all show up to help. They come drivin' up in a big Ford four-wheel-drive pickup, a deer guard on the front, mud and snow all around, a couple of spare tires tied to the stock racks, and a Handyman jack wired in the back of that hummer rattlin' like a beer can in a fifty-gallon drum! In the back of every one of them pickups is, at least, one GOOD dog! And two pups!

Now them dogs leap out and commence to fight with one another for two hours! You spend the rest of the day kickin' 'em out from under yer feet or chasin' 'em outta the gate!

But you can't say nothin'. Oh, no! That's a sacred thing! You can't criticize another man's dog!

Now everybody's got a dog story. Claude had spent all mornin' gettin' a bull off the mountain and was easin' 'im down toward a trap in the meadow. Tom came drivin' up and got out to open the corral gate. Ring leaped out of Tom's pickup and proceeded to put the bull back up the mountain.

Ring come trottin' back, lolling his tongue, a satisfied look on his face. You could almost hear him sayin', "Aren't you proud of me, Dad?" But one look at Claude's face, and you could hear Ring thinkin', Uh-oh!

Claude took Ring by the collar and proceeded to reenact the Olympic hammer throw event!

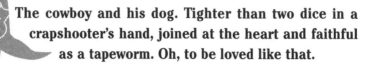

All over cow country these dingos, blue heelers, and Border collies go by similar names—Banjo, Badger, Penny, Bingo, Blue, Dally, or Dog—but under stress most of 'em git called the same thing! It's a term of endearment that refers to their maternal lineage!

There's probably a heaven for cowdogs where they can sit out on the edge of a cloud and look down at the earth. If atmospheric conditions are just right, they can cock an ear and hear some ol' cowboy yellin', "Go git in the pickup, you pot licker!"

Say it ain't so, Sweetie.

SCORPION STRIKES AGAIN

Dear Baxter,

I've been meaning to send you a thank-you for the new book you sent at Christmas. We have it about half colored, ha, ha.

I had it on my list of things to do today but I didn't get a chance. Charlie got stung by a scorpion, and he's really having a tough time metabolizing the venom. I had to be the nurse while he went through the numb and tinglies, wobbly eyes, and slobbers. In any case, it wasn't life threatening, just inconvenient.

We'd returned from church and lunch in town. Charlie took the Sunday paper and retired to the bathroom. I was in the laundry room when I heard a scream, really more like a duck call. When I went into the bathroom to see what was wrong, Charlie was crouched in front of the stool like an offensive lineman, trousers around his ankles, and wincing. Really wincing.

There was one teed off scorpion doing laps in the water. As near as we can tell, Mr. Scorpion had been on the back side of the couple squares of toilet paper that hung down from the roll. Charlie didn't see it, and it didn't see him until it was too late.

Since Charlie's brother and father both swear by the idea of shocking a scorpion sting or snakebite, and tell of their personal experiences willingly, I offered to go get the cattle prod from the barn to see if it would help if we shocked him a good one.

Charlie said he didn't care if it would restore baldness, induce labor, or cure bog spavin in horses, he would not stand still for Hot-Shot therapy. I then offered a kinder, gentler alternative. Since cold was supposed to help a sting, I would get him a bowl of ice cubes and a tong. He could place a cube on the sting with the tongs and clinch till it melted. He didn't go for that, either.

Before the kids left for school the next morning, he made us promise not to tell anyone exactly where he was stung. I can tell you that it's pretty hard, when asked that question, to keep a straight face and say, "In the bathroom."

Anyway, he's doing better, but he's developed a morbid fear of Mr. Whipple.

Our best to your family and thanks again for the book.

—Sweetie

HOMELESS DOGS

I passed a professional homeless person again today. She's staked out a corner at an intersection off the freeway that I take to go to the airport on a regular basis. She's a celebrity of sorts. I've seen at least two feature stories including her in the last year. She lives with a couple other homeless folks outside the city. They sleep in a car. According to the story, they are ex-alcoholics. But she's at her spot almost every morning before daylight, on her corner by the stop sign. She has a cardboard sign that asks for a handout because she's out of work and needs help and "God Bless."

Let me tell ya, she's not out of work. She's on duty on her corner regular as an insulin shot. She probably puts in more hours than the average consultant.

Did I mention she has a dog? She always has a dog with her. On cool winter mornings, his head is peeking out from under the nondescript blanket that she herself is wrapped in.

I used to think the dog was a ploy for sympathy. It would be a good one. Authors, movie producers, animal rights groups, and charities of all kinds have shamelessly used animals as a sympathy device.

But hers is not an easy life. Anybody who puts in 8 to 5, six days a week, knows that some mornings the drudgery can weigh you down. However, it makes it more bearable for most of us knowing we've got supper, the Barcalounger, sixty-four channels, and a clean warm bed waiting after we get off work. I'm not sure what she has waiting for her when she gets off work. I guess I don't want to think about it.

After giving her a couple bucks the first few times I passed, I began to resent her. Go git a job. Show a little self-respect. Take some initiative, I thought.

But I have come to the conclusion that there are people in society who just don't fit in. Where would she ever get a job?

I wouldn't hire her. Maybe she's emotionally unstable, mentally dysfunctional, antisocial. Whatever she is, though, she isn't lazy. Oh, sure, maybe she goes back to her hobo camp after a hard day's begging and gripes about the cheapskates in their new BMWs with the windows rolled up. "One guy asked if I could change a five. Can you believe it! Ah, well, another day. Think I'll have a diet pop and prop my feet up in front of the fire. Come here, ol' dog."

Of late, I no longer think the dog is a ploy. He's probably her best friend—something, I suspect, she doesn't have in abundance. For her, like a lot of us, her dog lends some kindness and comfort in an often unsympathetic world. The dog, in return, gets her love and protection.

Yup, she may be homeless, but her dog isn't.

Norman Maclean wrote some of the most beautiful words concluding one of his stories: "All existence fades to a being with my soul and memories and the sounds of the Big Blackfoot River and a four-count rhythm and the hope that a fish will rise. Eventually, all things merge into one, and a river runs through it."*

My apologies to Norman.

A POND RUNS THROUGH IT

It's not uncommon for cattle farmers to keep livestock ponds stocked with fish. In the Midwest, bass are considered the primo catch. Penny and her husband often take their guests out to the pond, but they are more sophisticated fishermen than most. They have outgrown the crude, clunking lures, the simulated plastic worms, the ticky-tacky spinners, and the oh-so-amateur refrigerated night crawlers.

They are fly fishermen.

Their friend John is a fly-fishing aficionado and a frequent guest. One afternoon, Penny walked with him across the pasture to the pond. They strode with the confidence of Olympic athletes. They competed, not against each other but only against themselves.

John, the minimalist, went up the bank carrying all his tackle in his shirt pocket. Penny, the princess of preparedness, set her backpack on the ten-foot dirt edge of the half-full pond.

She laid out everything she would need neatly along the bank: four boxes of flies, sinkers, net, forceps, suntan lotion, bottled water, energy bars, creel, combination knife and

*From *A River Runs Through It* by Norman Maclean. University of Chicago Press.

scaler, bug spray, and wire cutters. She kept her feet dry and began back-casting, laying the line, reeling and pausing, ebbing and flowing, all in perfect rhythm to the lapping of the wavelets on the shore.

Her concentration was intruded upon by the feeling that she was not alone. She looked around to see forty curious Angus heifers looking over her fly-fishing inventory like single mothers at a yard sale. They were licking, nudging, drooling, stomping, and scattering woolies, nymphs, slug bugs, hellgrammites, sunscreen, and oatmeal raisin cookies along the beach.

Penny tried shooing them back, but it was like trying to shoo snow off the porch. They had her surrounded and were closing in. "John! John!" she kept calling, trying to get some help.

She was actually whacking heifers on the head with her bare hand whilst holding her rod above the milling crowd. John was steadily giving advice: "Move sideways! Stand tall! Stoop and run! Twist and shout!"

As Penny was maneuvering, one of the heifers stuck her head under the fishing line. It startled her! She began backing up. The line hooked on the round ear tag button on the backside. The crowd parted as Penny played the heifer like an eight-hundred-pound walleye.

"Keep yer tip up," encouraged John.

The heifer ducked and dived, breached and sounded, wiggled and shook until she finally broke free. "Wow," said John to the panting Penny, "that's sure the big one that got away!"

"Yeah," said Penny, "but we mostly just catch and release."

The direction the tub drains depends on where you live. I prefer clockwise.

VANISHING EAST

I received a letter from a journalist. She included several self-penned poems that wistfully celebrated the mountains, the big sky, and the cowboy. She said she was chronicling the vanishing West.

Humm . . . , I thought, does that mean the East has already vanished?

At what point did it happen, when the Indians sold Manhattan? When Kentucky became a state? When the Brooklyn Dodgers moved to Los Angeles?

And how does something like "the East" vanish? Can it move to Atlanta? Get eaten by locust hordes? Or get covered up like a landfill?

Carrying this thought forward, it is just a short philosophical step from "chronicling the vanishing West" to "saving" it. Except that the ideas rise proportionally to Preposterous, on the lunatic scale. There are those who have proposed depopulating the Great Plains from Colorado to North Dakota and establishing a buffalo common. Others who support draining Lake Powell.

However, saving the West almost always entails eliminating any type of private enterprise, i.e., cattle, timber, mining, and fast-food franchises. According to the advocates, people should only be allowed to live in places like Flagstaff, Missoula, Aspen, and Palm Springs if they can be supplied essentials from elsewhere. Like living in Antarctica or on the moon.

But is it still possible to "save the East"? By definition, that would mean it should be returned to its pre-Pilgrim state.

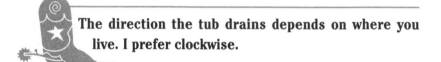

This would involve removing all commerce from the Chesapeake Bay and Boston Harbor. Eliminate those preying on tourists in Atlantic City and Nantucket. Reintroducing mountain lions, wolves, and grizzly bears in Gettysburg, Albany, and Washington, D.C., planting endangered species in Lake Ontario, and establishing plover and seagull commons on Long Island. A massive undertaking.

So, has the East really vanished, or should my journalist pen pal retreat to Baltimore to do her chronicling while there is still time? And more important, can we still save the East, or must we be stoic, keep one eye pointed toward the sunset, and march on lest we glance back like Lot's wife, and turn into a pillar of salt?

To their credit, the people from the TV channel wrote me a thoughtful response. I still haven't seen a feature on how to cut up a chicken or dehorn a goat, but maybe that's too "real life."

DEAR ANIMAL PLANET

Dear Animal Planet,

You have a great channel on cable TV. Many of the shows are fascinating and informative. However, there is a conspicuous absence of the most indispensable animals on the planet: domestic livestock.

Part of your popularity is the emphasis on human-animal bonding. You present animals, glamorous or otherwise, as creatures worthy of our esteem. You even use animals as comedians, straight men, fall guys, victims, sports figures, teachers, actors, singers, and commercial spokescritters. It is a cornucopia of Disney-like anthropomorphism, using live animals instead of cartoons.

But you also show death on the Serengeti. Exposing city children to the simple act of a cheetah kill is essential if they are to ever understand the order of existence on earth. It has been a part of life since omnivores entered the food chain.

So I would suggest that including related stories about domestic animals and the people who care for them would be an easy step. Ninety-seven percent of our population eats meat. Yet most urban kids have no idea where it comes from. Modern society has separated the ham from the burger, the chicken from the nugget, and the hot fudge sundae from the holstein.

We have sanitized our children's world. So they can eat without considering the sacrifice and service that domestic animals provide to humans' well-being. For those who might think urban people are not capable of dealing with the blunt truth of animal production, I suggest that they are. From the beginning of civi-

lization until fifty years ago, the majority of the earth's population was agriculturally cognizant. People learned from childhood the intricate intimacy of raising and dealing with livestock.

Country kids still maintain this close natural relationship. It instills respect and a sacred responsibility toward those animals in their care who are destined for the food chain. Conversations with these country kids would open a world of understanding to an audience largely insulated from this fundamental part of their real life.

When my daughter was eleven years old, we were raising rabbits. She was showing a new litter to her urban aunt. "They're so cute," said Aunt. "What will you do with them?"

"When they're about five pounds, we sell them to the grocery store," she replied.

Her aunt was aghast! "How can you do that!" she blurted.

My eleven-year-old looked up at her and said, "I don't make friends with them."

Wisdom as ancient as time from the mouth of a child. It could be useful on Animal Planet.

The continuing saga of the city mouse and the country mouse.

NEW NEIGHBORS

Country versus Urban—the rubbing of cultural tectonic plates.

Mike is a rancher in that beautiful-to-look-at country of central Oregon. His ranch house is set back from the road, fronted by a lush irrigated pasture.

In the green flush of late spring, sprinkled with colorful bovines, backdropped by verdant pines, porcelain-white clouds and china-blue sky, the setting is pretty as a picture. Perfect for developers promoting nearby "ranchette estates."

Hot on the trail of peace and serenity—straight from the five-speed, fuel-injected, Teflon-encased, pre-taste-tested coast of central California came the new urban next-door neighbor.

Gushing and garrulous, he descended on Mike one afternoon as he labored at irrigating the roadside pasture that bordered both their front yards.

The new neighbor, hereinafter referred to as Sherman, was deeply impressed by the cows and how beautiful they looked in the overall pasture setting. He liked that he could see them from his living room window. Sherman had been in the "art world" before he began networking web pages and appreciated Mike's cow color selections.

"The russet and beige offset the licorice and peppermint so well. They look like Christmas candy in an Easter basket," he opined. "I hope you don't mind if I befriend them?"

They parted, Sherman walking on air and Mike scratching his head.

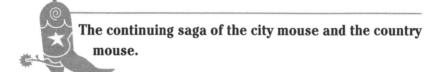

The following week a big ruckus ensued when Mike found half his cows out on the highway. Tracking them back home, he found the break in the fence. It was a hundred yards long and ran across the front of Sherman's lawn. The posts and wire were gone!

"What were you thinking?" asked the incredulous Mike.

"Oh, don't worry," said Sherman excitedly. "I've bought a beautiful three-pole, drilled-and-doweled pine log fence to put in its place. It'll be here in a couple of weeks."

"Well, what are we gonna use in the meantime to keep the cows off the road?"

"Don't you have some fence we can use temporarily?"

"I did," said Mike, "but you took it all down. Where is it?"

"I gave it to my brother-in-law to use for his horse. The green posts and silvery wire complement his Appaloosa better than your cows." Sherman put an arm around Mike's shoulder. "Come in the house, and I'll show you my plans for redecorating your barn."

JUST SAY NO!

- "My brother says it works everytime!"
- "I know Pinto took her out, but she's not that kind of a girl!"
- "Your wife will just love a new drill press!"
- "It's the cow deal of a lifetime, but I need a cosigner!"
- "It's not cleared for scours, and I can't officially recommend it, but . . ."
- "This will make you rich!"
- "The Japanese eat it this way all the time!"
- "The Indians ate it like this right after they killed the buffalo!"
- "I know his sire was a dwarf, but I don't think it's hereditary!"
- "I've got it on good authority they're going to rezone this property!"
- "Buy this guy in the calcutta. You've never heard of him, but he ropes good; he just doesn't travel much!"
- "The vet say's she'll settle in spite of how it looks!"
- "He just bumped it in the trailer!"
- "I know they look drawn, but think of the weighin' condition!"
- "I never turned a steer out on the place that didn't gain three hundred pounds!"
- "Yer right, it is the runt. But he's the smartest one of the litter!"
- "A little hot wire and you could run six hundred buffalo on this place!"
- "Sure I kin fix yer car. Kin I borry yer tools?"
- "If she's not in foal, I'll eat my hat!"
- "This aluminum gate comes with a lifetime guarantee!"

- "Why, the hunting lease will make the payments on this ol' ranch!"
- "I'll buy 'em back in the fall!"
- "No, I've never heard a horse bark like that before, either, but I don't think it's serious!"
- "And with this degree in economics you'll always be able to get a job!"
- "If you elect me . . ."

Old dogs don't age any more gracefully than most humans. We kinda draw into ourselves and spend a lot of time dreamin' about the good old days. Uncle Leonard, who died at ninety-four, said it best: "Why can't we lose our testicles and keep our teeth."

OL' ROOKIE'S FLASHBACK

Old dogs. They write songs about 'em and watermelon wine. They have sayings about 'em learning new tricks. They even name feet after them, i.e., "My ol' dogs are shore tired!"

In a dog's life span, they usually figure seven dog years equals one human year. Little dogs usually live longer than big dogs. Fourteen is old for a dog. Rookie turned fourteen this year.

Ol' Rookie is a good-sized spotted hound dog belonging to my friend Mac. I saw the two of them this summer. Mac was lookin' good; Rookie looked like a dyin' duck in a thunderstorm! He was drawn up and pore. He panted and gazed into space a lot of the time. He had trouble getting up and down. He stumbled over Popsicle sticks and tumblebugs.

We thought he was so deaf, he couldn't hear himself bark. But after closer observation, we noticed that when you called him, ol' Rookie would look the other way. I reckon he was just ignoring us. A privilege we grant older folks of any species.

He practiced "snappin flies." Only trouble was, after they'd been snapped, he'd open his mouth and the fly would buzz out lazily. Rookie didn't have many teeth left, ya see.

He had fleas, ticks, and a squadron of flies that hovered over him like groupies around a rock star. I suggested we give him a bath and hang an insecticide ear tag on his collar. Mac said he'd considered that, but he was afraid the ol' dog would be lonesome. I didn't understand. He said ol' Rookie is packin' his own peanut gallery!

He'd doze off in the shade of a tree, then sit up suddenly and start barking. Then he'd look around with a puzzled expression and flop back down in the grass. Barkin' at old memories.

I saw him walk out to the road and visit with a Doberman female. They sniffed, and I saw his tail wag a little and a silly grin slide across his ol' gray muzzle. I said, "Look at that. He's still got fire in the furnace!"

Mac glanced at his longtime canine pardner and said, "Don't get yer hopes up. I think ol' Rookie's just havin' a flashback."

When I moved from Idaho to Colorado, I had quit my job, lost my house, car, horse, trailer, and first wife. The man takin' over my veterinary job at the feedlot inherited my pickup. He took me to the airport and dropped me at the curb. "Have you got everything?" I looked down at my duct-taped guitar case and hangin' bag. I felt my pockets, "Wait," I said, "I forgot my keys, I . . ." I paused as it sunk in. I was down to no keys.

DOWN TO NO KEYS

I was visitin' with an ol' *capacho* the other day. We were talkin' 'bout bein' down to no keys. I said, "Pardner, have you ever been down and out?" "Down!" he said. "I been down so low I could count the spots on a lizard's belly!"

I said, "How'd ya git by?" He said, "When you got a lotta time to kill but no money to spend, well, let's say I developed some mighty cheap hobbies."

"Like what?" says I.

"Pickin' yer nose. When you have the time to spend, that can become a highly developed art form. In fact, it should be an Olympic event. And finding addresses of old friends who owe you money.

"Pickin' up roadkill . . . you can render possum grease and sell coon hides. You can spend a lot of time runnin' yer quail traps. I know fifteen different ways to line up cottontails so you can git two with one shot.

"I taught a wild turkey to fetch and a raven how to bark like a coyote. I know how to season navy beans with prickly pear and fifty recipes for sardines and Vienna sausage.

"I've spliced a million reins, hog-ringed my bit chains, and covered my horn with a nut sack just to git by. And a feller can spend a satisfyin' afternoon huntin' old horseshoes.

"You can resole your boots with cowhide, cardboard, sidewalls, or electrical tape. Many's the time I've straightened last year's straw hat.

"Some other cheap hobbies I've taken up are whittlin', straightenin' nails, cullin' socks, patchin' jeans, and rememberin'. Rememberin', you do that a lot.

"Summer evenin's is a good time to identify insects.

"If yer lucky enough to have an ol' truck, lots of time can be piddled away keepin' it runnin'. I've spent plenty of time figgerin' out which tire to use for a spare. A field trip to the wreckin' yard can be fun and productive. Lookin' for good spark plugs, lug nuts, and drain-plug pans. Or jackin' it up, collecting the motor oil, and letting it settle so you can use it again. Have you ever used tin foil for a head gasket?

"I learned to cut my own hair, drink the less expensive wines, and make a bag of Red Man last six weeks."

"Gosh," I said, "you oughta write a book!"

"I can't," said he. "Too busy. This afternoon I'm goin' through my old razor blades; what the sociologists call quality time."

Team roping is my hobby, but the ability to toss a loop around a beast and handle it is an asset in veterinary medicine. Matter of fact, a course in roping at veterinary school would have been more useful than the second semester of histology.

THE ROPIN' VET

Louie used to buy horses for the feedlot. Whenever he'd find a good stout one that was deaf and looked like it could tread mud, he'd send it our way. I'd usually check 'em over, float their teeth, worm 'em, vaccinate 'em, and change their oil. Occasionally he sent one with no faults, but I was only there ten years, so I never saw him!

Feedlot #3 called one morning to say Louie'd delivered a new horse to the yard. As I pulled up to the horse barn, I called Louie on the radio to ask about any "peculiarities." I'd learned from past experience that all arrived with a flaw of some kind . . . some minor, some fatal.

"Louie, what can you tell me 'bout the new horse?"

"You'll like him, Doc. Gentle as a puppy. Sound, maybe twelve years old, big'un . . . sixteen hands. Belonged to a little old lady who only rode him to the senior center once a week."

I waited.

"Oh, by the way, he's a little hard to catch."

In the first pen stood ol' Whitey. He had a gentle look in his eye. I walked right up to him. He backed off. I coaxed, wheedled, cooed, and clucked him 'round and 'round the corral.

Now, as any vet can tell ya, I didn't hire on to train 'em! Just to doctor 'em!

I ran outta patience, threw down the halter, and got out my rope! Although there are exceptions, most vets are not good ropers. It's like givin' a typewriter to a cephalopod! I roped the post, the hay rack, the back rubber, the barn door, the two horses with Whitey, and finally caught him in midair jumping the water tank!

Years later, I still haven't learned my lesson. To this day, I carry a rope and act like I can use it!

Dr. Huey down in Tennessee is smarter'n me. He went out to look at an ol' tobacco farmer's sick calf.

"He's in the pasture, Doc. I'm busy but you're young. You can catch him."

Huey dug his rope outta the truck and started swingin' it. He knocked the ol' man's hat off before it finally hung on the pickup mirror.

"You any good with that?" asked the ol' man suspiciously.

"Not too, but it don't make any difference to me," says Huey. "I charge a dollar a throw whether I catch 'em or not!"

The ol' man yelled over his shoulder, "Leroy, git out there and catch that calf for the good doctor!"

The cowboy girl . . . unsung in history but never silenced.

GEORGE AND ELLIE

I saw Ellie and George at the feed store the other day. She was wearing a walking cast on her left leg. She'd broken the dorsal tip of her fibula and pulled some tendons. It was the result of her perverse need to train young horses.

She was in pain and George was despondent. She couldn't drive, so he had to haul her to town every day to do errands. I remarked that she was the luckiest woman in the world to have an attentive and thoughtful man like him to wait on her hand and foot.

He agreed and had formulated a workout program for her so that she wouldn't feel completely useless. Another sign of his deep concern for her holistic well-being.

He had been devoting considerable mental energy tryin' to figger out the easiest way for her to open gates. It seemed to him that's what she missed the most.

I asked him how she got in the truck. He said he backed up to the loading chute and pushed her in with a wheelbarrow. He'd throwed a couple bales of straw in the back for her comfort.

And gettin' out? I asked. Easy as backin' in the old chicken house and lettin' her grab one of the low-hangin' rafters. He said it worked pretty good the second time after he'd repaired the crossbeam.

I wasn't sure I understood how she managed to open the gate from the pickup bed. He said that was one of the drawbacks. He had to back everywhere he went. And she still had trouble with wire gates.

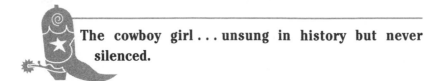

How 'bout a big ramp of some kind, I suggested. She could drop it off the end of the tailgate and slide down. Maybe tie a piece of cotton rope to the gooseneck ball and pull herself back up.

He'd already thought of that, he answered, but it took her too long to drag herself around the pickup and back. Not to mention the dirt and gravel that collected in her cast.

"As we speak," he informed me, "I'm workin' on a new idea. Jack is weldin' me a small A-frame with a boom on it. It'll bolt to my front bumper. We're gonna hang an ol' truck tire by a chain on the boom. She'll be able to swing sideways from one headlight to the other, open and close any gate I can get up to."

He'd fixed her up with a pushin' pole and a gaff hook. "Should work slick as a whistle," he said. "She can do it all by herself. Have a sense of accomplishment."

"And you won't have to get out of the pickup," I added.

"Yup," he said, "I do what I have to to build her self-esteem."

We're talkin' abnormal affection here.

EDSEL'S TRUCK

They say that dogs often take on the behavior of their owners. Chuck loved old vehicles, especially trucks. They rusted pretty quick in the heat and humidity of southeast Texas, so finding one whose body was in good shape was like striking gold.

His wife, Judy, didn't mind his harmless collecting. The ranch had lots of places to park old trucks, and his hobby was a reliable source of amusement for her over the years.

Enter Edsel. A year-old German shepherd pup who could not pass the rigid registered-breed physical exam. He showed a tendency to hip dysplasia, and his ears would not stand up straight. The softhearted breeder had him neutered and gave him to Chuck, who gave him the name in honor of that crack in Ford Motor Company's good judgment that had a life span shorter than a cream pie in a food fight.

Edsel adopted Chuck's love for old vehicles. He and Chuck would walk out to the pasture littered with molding REOs, IHs, Studebakers, Caminos, Model A's, Power Wagons, and Chevys. They would pull open a door and climb up in the cab with its bare springs, crystallized glass, wooden crates, and grass growing up through the floorboards. They covered many an imaginary mile on quiet afternoons.

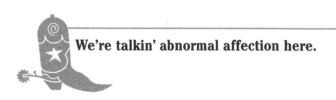

One day, they had a visitor in a sleek, racy, low-slung Cadillac DeVille. The ranch driveway was gravel with water-diverting speed bumps. They parked in front of the house and came in. Seeking muffler contact or warmth or shade, who knows, Edsel crawled underneath the Caddy. When the visitors went to leave, they heard a yowl! Thinking they had hit a dog, they jumped out. They had managed to high-center Edsel between the car and the speed bump. He couldn't budge. It took a bumper jack and two Vienna sausages to get him out from under.

Chuck came home one day with a "fairly good" 1940 black Ford pickup, with the intention of fixing it up. Edsel shared his enthusiasm. Although the windshield was out and it wouldn't run, the wheels still turned and the hood ornament was intact. Dear Judy refused to be persuaded to join him, but Chuck would have his son chain up the old Ford with his tractor and pull him around the yard. Actually, out on the highway occasionally. Judy said it was a sight to see: Chuck at the wheel, smiling serenely, and Edsel in the passenger seat, tongue lolling, nostrils flaring, and ears blown straight up in the steady breeze as they circled past the kitchen window, around and around. Edsel developed a deep attachment to the truck. He began sleeping in it and storing bones in the bed.

Alas, one day, a neighbor took a liking to the '40 Ford and offered Chuck more than it was worth. The problem of the dog came up. They worked it out. Chuck retained joint custody and visitation rights, and Edsel stayed with the truck. And, until Edsel went to dog heaven, on pretty afternoons you might see a tractor pulling an old '40 Ford pickup down a Harris County road with a man and a dog ensconced in the seat, a picture of contentment. Out on a date, some might say.

JACKSON HOLE FIRES

Nature is relentless—sooner or later it bites you in the backside and takes back its own.

That's what kept running through my mind as I listened to dramatic reports of forest fires threatening multimillion-dollar homes in the Jackson Hole, Wyoming, area. What a tragedy it would have been had any firefighters been injured or killed defending those homes.

It is the casual arrogance of modern man that allows us to build in floodplains, forested plots, sandy beaches, earthquake faults, tornado alleys, and lava flows.

In ancient history, man built in dangerous places but often out of ignorance. Nowadays, we intrude ourselves on risky ground, fully informed of the danger. Yet we blithely charge on like the Russian roulette player.

One cannot criticize the need for humans to expand and settle. And natural catastrophes can occur anywhere on the planet. Yet it does seem that common sense eludes many of our choices. Our ego overrides the wisdom of old-timers.

These last two decades have seen an influx of suburban dwellers moving to the country. Many quiet rural communities have been "invaded" by city folks seeking a more pastoral environment. But rather than fit in, they wind up rebuilding their previous environment, which is mostly concrete malls, fast food, Wal-Marts, and theaters. They have an expectation of the protective, service-oriented technology to insulate them from inconvenience, even if their property is only a summer home.

And, it's not such a bad thing, this trickle-down decadence. The original residents of these rural communities benefit. They like having an espresso or "TCBY" now and then. But there was a reason bear hunting was allowed, roads were closed in winter, the swamp was drained, they all had cellars, or brush was cleared. And no one built houses in the bottom of the arroyo, on the mudslide hill, or in the deep woods.

I'm sure those homeowners in Jackson Hole were warned . . . *not* by the real estate developers, the chamber of commerce, or contractors, but by the spit-and-whittle seasoned natives who live in trailer houses, ranches, and thirty-year-old houses in town.

So when the big fire came, the new homeowners were the only ones who were surprised, and, as usual, their expensive ill-placed monuments to modern man's arrogance were saved to burn another day.

Which, some might say is inevitable, unless they can start paving the area right away. Because, although nature does bide its time, it is relentless. However, this summer's lesson will not go completely unlearned. I expect we will see some of these homes on the market soon, as soon as they can get the smoke out of the curtains.

Being raised in Las Cruces, New Mexico, and presently living forty miles from the *frontera* in Arizona, I am steeped in the Mexican culture. Furthermore, making my living in agriculture, I can appreciate the immigrants' enormous contribution to the "cheap food" policy closely guarded and maintained by the U.S. Congress. These workers are responsible for more than just the jalapeños in our cornucopia.

HISPANIC AGRICULTURE

"I'm concerned that more Hispanics aren't going into agriculture as a profession." So spoke my old friend Buddy, who is Hispanic himself. He was president of the state Ag Chemical Association. He has three grown children, none of whom show any interest in their dad's or granddad's agricultural livelihoods.

I have given this phenomenon much thought since our discussion, and I keep coming back to the same reason for it: Maybe most Hispanics associate agriculture with hoes. They want to be as far from the reminders that their parents, grandparents, or great-greats came across the border and spent their lives in toil.

In a recent survey of the one hundred most influential Hispanics in American business, 77 percent of which were descended from Mexico and Cuba, not a single one had an agricultural affiliation. Over 50 percent were included in government; the majority of the rest were evenly divided between corporate business or were entrepreneurs. These findings certainly confirm Buddy's assertions.

I grew up in the Southwest. My home county is 65 percent Spanish-speaking. I have a great respect for Mexican immigrants, legal or illegal. They have traits I admire: ambition, bravery, self-control, stamina, and a desire to improve their condition. I like to think if I was trapped in hopeless class prej-

DAVE HOLL

udice and economic oppression, I'd climb a wall or swim a river, too.

Mexican labor has been the backbone of southwestern agriculture for centuries. As it has been for every other race of immigrant people, it is the first generation in a family that bears most of the burden and suffers the perils, the drudgery, the fear, and prejudice.

Even today, Mexican immigrants are mostly poor rural people. The skills they possess include a feel for land and stock, dirt, water, and produce. It is natural for them to seek work they are accustomed to.

A regular or even seasonal paycheck at minimum wage here in the land of plenty can make them rich men back in their hometowns in Mexico. Should they choose to stay and raise their families here, they can earn a decent living. But they hope for a better life for their children. They send them to school and insist they speak English.

Yet, as Buddy says, rarely do these descendants pursue an occupation in the business where their ancestors have had such a great impact.

America today is becoming a service-oriented society. It does not place much value on farming, mining, or timber occupations. Matter of fact, it looks down on any job that involves manual labor.

But any farmer or cowboy can tell you it is honorable work that requires skill and gets hands dirty. What is more manual than scooping a bunk, shoeing a horse, building a fence, blocking beets, or picking oranges?

Maybe with many Mexican Americans, the memory of pickin' cotton is too fresh. But like Buddy, I agree that American agriculture could benefit from the now bilingual, educated, assimilated descendants of Señores Juan, Tomas, José, and Maria, who gave them a start.

Agriculture for them offers more than just blisters and sore backs. Abuelito already paid that price.

This was written more than a decade ago. It's sad that it's still topical.

ETHIOPIA, WHY ME?

Ethiopia is a long way from here. Besides, I don't know a single Ethiopian. And, I've been busy. I haven't had much time to think about Ethiopia. How 'bout you? We've got a lot on our minds. We're tryin' to make ends meet.

Ya know, it's hard for me to imagine anyone starving to death. I admit I've seen it, but only rarely, in animals. The body's fat begins to go to work on its own protein stores. Stuff like muscles. Muscular power and activity decrease as the body continues to burn itself up to survive. The skeleton and heart muscles are about the last thing to go. Death is usually due to heart failure. But, like I said, I've never seen it in people.

I've seen pictures, though. Lots of 'em from Ethiopia. Lethargic, bloated children. Skinny adults with no hope in their eyes. I think they print those pictures to get my sympathy.

Then they run commercials showing happy diners, smacking their lips and not cleaning their plate. Then they cut to a shot of a walking skeleton: no hair, lots of flies on the person's face. You've seen 'em. It's always a child, did you notice?

Course, they are always asking for money. Send it here, send it there; all for the starving children. How do we know it's not siphoned off by bureaucratic middlemen? How do we know it even gets to the children?

Sounds like the Ethiopians have had a run of bad luck. They need a little rain. I guess some of us know about that. Why, some of us have even applied for drought relief.

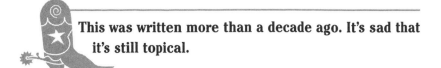

Who are these Ethiopians? Are they all starving? There must be some fat ones. Probably the ones in the front of the line—the ones doling out the wheat. They live in a country that is almost as big as Texas and Iowa put together. It is a communist country but one of the prominent religions is Christianity. In Africa, no less. I hadn't realized that.

It's getting harder and harder to ignore Ethiopia. Commentator movie stars, singers, politicians, columnists, and yer run-of-the-mill do-gooders keep throwing it in our faces.

What do they expect me to do—help?

This commentary was written at the beginning of America's war on terrorism, shortly after we had begun attacking the Taliban forces in Afghanistan. The UN was also airlifting tons of food aid. The incongruity of dropping food and medical supplies to the natives while bombing the country struck me as odd.

It once again put American agriculture on the front page.

FOOD AID TO AFGHANISTAN

Allow me to quote Yar Mohamed, Afghani soldier: "We will never surrender bin Laden. . . . We will do everything for the safety and security of our guest."

Reminded of the thousands of tons of grain being shipped into his starving country by the UN, most of which is being donated by the American government, he dismissed the food aid by saying, "It is the politics of America."

Ain't it ever? The beefed-up, months-early farm bill steamrolled through the House over President Bush's objection. Politicians know, our allies know, even our enemies know . . . that our agricultural bounty, the sweat and soil, the seed and toil, the abundant dirt cheap life-sustaining daily bread is the cornerstone of politics in America.

One strategy to win a war is to starve the enemy. So why are we willing to pour food aid into the cauldron of Taliban territory in the midst of the fighting? Self-defeating, some would say. I suspect it is based on the conviction that Yar, in his fanatic loyalty, would be willing to starve himself for the cause, but *Mrs.* Yar may not be quite so willing to starve her children to prove a point.

Once again America charges into the breech of conflict with butter and breadsticks.

Politicians, even more than generals, know that if your weapons are edible, one must have a ready supply of ammunition. Thus, the current emphasis on the new farm bill.

President Bush is concerned that it will stimulate overproduction. Congress knows it will. Overproduction is the basis of the cheap-food policy encouraged by Congress since God invented supply and demand.

This time, however, no one will be griping about "subsidized farming." We expect to have to feed hundreds of thousands of Muslim refugees during our war on terrorism. And no one doubts that American farmers will rise to the occasion.

There is no promise to producers that they will be paid more than the subsistence prices they are paid now. But for the time being that doesn't matter. As Yar says, "Food aid is the politics of America."

So the flags flying across the fruited plain from our barns and combines, our tractors and saddlehorns will be a sign to Mrs. Yar that if the farmers have anything to do about it, her children will not starve to death in her arms while our brother soldiers go about excising the cancers of the civilized world.

This one ran on NPR Christmas Day, 2001. America had soldiers in harm's way in Afghanistan. Flags were flying across the country; President Bush had an 88 percent approval rating; and many of us felt a renewed sense of communal affection.

It was also a time of reflection for many baby boomers, me included. It stimulated a mixed bag of mail.

EMPTY PLACES AT THE CHRISTMAS TABLE

This Christmas, I am filled with a deep sense of respect for my father and brother, Grandpa Tommy, Thurman, Wayne, Foxy, Clovis, Pinto, Jim, Danny, and their thousands and thousands of comrades who have gone to war.

This holiday season, as in too many in our lifetime, there will be empty places around the Yuletide table for sons and daughters in the service of our country.

In my mind, soldiers—perhaps because I never was one—hold a mystical image: knights, rifles, battered banners, gun smoke, charging horses, tanks, glory, honor, and courage.

Vietnam was my war. I was never drafted, I didn't volunteer. I regret it. During that time I held Jane Fonda and the deserters to Canada in contempt. Yet, was I any better than they if I never served?

Since September 11, there has been a significant reversal in the attitude of the public toward our soldiers. From a suspicious, distanced acceptance to an almost gushing admiration. It is easy to have an impersonal relationship with "the military" if you think of them as professional robots in uniform. But when we see our family, friends, and neighbors' kids enlisting, we remember that ours is an army of everyday citizens serving for a short time, doing their duty. And that they will be back, most of them, and we will be better off because they went.

I grew up in the era of war protesters; I see them appearing now, still receiving lots of media attention. I guess it's a good thing, in a way. They can be a barometer of the battle. Because they'll always have the right to protest . . . as long as we are winning.

Patriotism is a personal realization that there is a greater calling than your own self-interest. Divisive and bickering as we can be among ourselves, when our family is threatened, we can be a fearsome foe.

This new war is different. We are fighting ruthless back-shooters, and they have our children in their crosshairs. It is hard to be blasé when you see soldiers with automatic weapons on the concourse at the Kansas City Airport.

Our government's response has been swift and massive with the overwhelming support of Americans. I have no doubt we will prevail.

I hope and pray that our knights in armor will slay the terrorist dragon and return victorious to sit with us at the Christmas table very soon.

Go git 'em, doughboys. Yo mama, Osama! I wish I could go with ya.

There are places on earth where living does not come easy. Places with harsh environments that most people would not do well in: parts of North Dakota, Nevada, Maine, Arizona, Oregon, or Louisiana. The Great Plains with its blizzards, droughts, tornadoes, and constant breath-stealing wind can drive people to the edge, too. All you can do is stand and take it, because it's not gonna give in.

HARDY TREES

Shade don't come easy on the high plains. It takes a pretty hardy tree to survive.

It is no place for the oak, the maple, or the stately sycamore. Though these trees are imposing and grand, they are cripplingly dependent. They are like corporate purchasing agents. Powerful and catered to only as long as their lifeline remains intact. In the case of these trees, they require a constant supply of water in vast quantities.

As long as it rains, they stand tall and live long, resistant to the puny encroachments of bugs, woodpeckers, and real estate developers. They have the strength of iron.

But survival in a land where rain is dear requires a different kind of strength. The ability to bend without breaking, stretch without snapping. To shrivel and wither, then spring back pliable and sinewy when exposed to water. Their strength is that of rawhide.

I saw a photograph in a magazine of an old gas station. The photographer was trying to capture a nostalgic feeling. The horizon behind the station was flat, and the ground was dusty. The only thing green was the elm tree.

It could have been in Perryton, Texas, Philip, South Dakota, Grover, Colorado, or a million other places where trees are not taken for granted.

Elm trees probably came with the settlers. They took root and made many a squatter's nest a home. They lined the streets in towns that were to be. They staked a claim for civilization.

Nowadays, lots of folks consider the elm tree a pest, a "trash tree." They are exterminated from well-kept lawns where the flowering ash and weeping willow are given a manicured stage. And for good reason. Elm trees send out suckers. They have lots of deadfall. They shed, pollinate, and break. They are susceptible to beetles, fungus, and horses. Some might say they are ugly and have outlived their usefulness.

But, ya know, it's hard to kill an elm tree. I've even taken to planting them around my place. I kinda admire something that can take everything God and man can throw at 'em and still keep comin'.

Shade don't come easy on the high plains. It takes a pretty hardy people to survive.

It's a wonder no one gets hurt out here!

GIMP

I was out in the driveway scattering stove ash when I heard the geese. It was three days until the end of the season, and I was still 0 for 6. They rose from the field to the north, squawking raucously and aiming straight over the house.

I dropped the coal bucket in the snow and raced back in the front door! I careened off the furniture like a bad billiard shot! At the back door, I grabbed the big twelve gauge leaning against the wall and three shells that I had conveniently placed on the top of the window ledge. Crashing off the back porch, I loaded the gun with the relaxed ease of a thirteen-year-old on his first date! The geese beat the air above me as I swung the shotgun skyward. Boom! Boom! The geese sailed over the barn like a giant manta ray. Nary a feather fluttered to the ground, but my two horses thundered from the barn!

I was in a funk that evening when I went to feed. But I noticed that my new rope horse was packin' his right hind. After a thorough lameness exam, I concluded he musta slid on the ice and pulled a muscle. Possibly, I admitted, the result of a sudden fright.

Join the club. My old dog, Boller, was favoring his left front. Considering his long history of bein' shot and run over, I wasn't surprised.

The cat Lefty got stepped on a couple years ago, and the doc amputated her right hind.

Adding my bilateral bursitis, Dionicio's bad back, and my teenager's loss of memory, my place looks like a World War I field hospital. It's a hazard of country life.

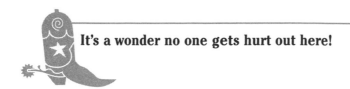

My friend Charlie has a cowdog named Gimp. Charlie has established a breeding program and now has produced a litter of pups that all limp. He wrote me of his success, predicting that he will make a million selling them to cowmen. His theory is that it will save an enormous amount of time getting a cowdog to the bum leg-ged stage.

And, he stressed, it is humane, since they won't have to go through the agony of getting injured in the first place. He says that a gimpy dog will be more cautious around kicking cows, truck tires, bangin' chutes, and cattle alleys. They can get right down to business.

It might be a good idea, but Charlie, like me, is gettin' a little long in the tooth. We're getting too practical. Playin' it safe. Goin' to bed early and eating our prunes. We're thinkin' like old dogs.

Young dogs think work is play. They turn over a new rock every day as they discover their world. Kinda like the thrill I got when I saw those geese fill the sky. Innocent wonderment. Made me feel like a puppy again.

Like I said, it's a wonder no out gets hurt out here!

COWHIDE ON THE SOLES OF HIS BOOTS

I wanna tell y'all a true story that happened to a friend of mine. Big Jim was judgin' the rodeo at Burlington last year. They call him Big Jim 'cause he's big as a round bale and twice as tough. But he don't move quite as fast as he did in his ol' bronc-ridin' days.

Big Jim's always had a way with animals. He roped a skunk one time when he was a little boy and drug it home. His dad made him unsaddle a hundred yards from the house. Jim said his ol' pony walked right into the pond and stuck his whole head under the water . . . several times. He finally sold the saddle. Two years later. In the winter.

They claim he and his dog, Pat, cornered a three-hundred-pound wild boar in a thicket unarmed and did him in with his Barlow.

So Big Jim is used to animals behavin' peculiar around him.

The stock contractor told Jim that his blue mare would buck out and come round to the right. Jim positioned himself to see when the saddle bronc rider marked 'er out. The rider called for the horse.

Out they came, pitchin' and rollin'. The cowboy was spurrin' fer all he was worth, and the ol' mare was feelin' her oats. She bucked toward Big Jim. He backed up. She kept comin' toward him. He kept backin' up till he was backed up against the front of the chute.

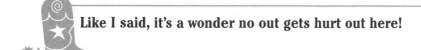

Ol' Blue stuck her head right against Big Jim's chest and pinned him to the fence! She had her mouth wide open and was squealin' like a cheerleader at the high school basketball finals. She was strikin' and pawin' and flailin' on both sides of his rigid body. Splinters and sparks were flyin' off both sides of Big Jim's head.

He daren't move a muscle. He was less than three feet from the dumbfounded bronc stomper who was still spurrin' like a hound dog in a gopher hole! They were lookin' at each other with Pekingese eyes.

Silver and horsehair were flashin' and flyin' in furious strokes as the rider continued to try to impress the judge. It can be said that he certainly had his attention. This continued for a three-second eternity, then the mare fell back, wheeled, and mule-kicked at the petrified judge. Both hooves hit the chute simultaneously on each side of Jim's head at eye level. Then she bucked off down the arena.

The other judge come runnin' over. "Are ya OK? Could ya see what happened? Was he spurrin' on both sides? How'd ya mark 'im?"

"Wull," said Big Jim, "I know the kid's got the makin's of a bronc rider. He had his toes pointed out so far that from where I was standin', I could read 'genuine cowhide' on the soles of his boots!"

"Timed event" rodeo cowboys compete in the roping and bulldogging events. They must pull a horse trailer from rodeo to rodeo in order to compete. It takes more effort, but they consider themselves the rodeo elite. The bronc riders and bullriders are a more low-maintenance group and are not really sure what ropers do for fun.

TIMED EVENT MAN

In the world of rodeo, cowboys usually fall into one of two categories: rough stock riders or timed event men. Each looks on the other with suspicion. Bronc riders can't imagine havin' to drag a horse and trailer all over the country, and ropers think bull riding is uncivilized!

Jack and Russell entered the punkin roller at Bokchito, Oklahoma. They were both sixteen and invincible! On arrival, they discovered a mix-up. Jack was entered in the bareback and Russell in the calf roping. Jack complained, "I told Mr. Ward to put me in the calf ropin' and Russell was ridin' bares! Besides, Russell's bought a brand-new riggin'!" Which of course he had! Not only that, Russell had a new set of custom-made bronc spurs and had just attended Mel Autry's rodeo school!

The secretary glared at him and growled, "Well, Jack, you better see if it fits your hand, 'cause I ain't changin' the order!"

They stomped around cussing the contractor, the secretary, their luck, and each other's event. But as the eight-track played the national anthem, Jack was down in the chute tryin' to pound his left hand into Russell's right-hand riggin'!

Minnie Mouse was an eight-hundred-pound grulla mare. Jack made some comment about stick horses and Shetlands. 'Bout not wantin' to hurt her. Russell ignored him. Jack was sorta scratchin' his spurs a little and thinkin', By, gosh, this ain't bad! I'm winnin' the bareback! Easier than I thought.

At the quarter-mile pole, Minnie Mouse bogged her head, planted her front feet, and exploded in midair! By the time she lit on all fours again, Jack had both legs on the left side and was laid across her like a roll of carpet!

He couldn't get his hand free! With all his weight stickin' out like a wind vane on the starboard side, he began to drag the little mare right. From his vantage point on the wing tip, Jack could see the arena fence flashing by at eye level. He was stuck hard and fast and pulling her closer and closer. Big square ties and net wire began clickin' by like a railroad bed.

Gosh, he thought, I hope it's cheap wire. . . .

He needn't have worried. He hit a tie! The collision was so calamitous it knocked the mare down!

At the conclusion of this spectacular exhibition, the crowd applauded wildly. As Jack hobbled out the gate, a man in yellow boots and a bolo tie asked him where he was gonna be appearing next.

Standing in the parking lot after the rodeo, Jack observed what a sorry job Russell had done in the calf roping.

Russell studied his pardner. Jack's shirt flapped in tatters on his right shoulder. The off side of his head looked like somebody had hit him with a fourteen-inch rasp and his arms no longer hung symmetrically. Russell figgered the eyebrow would grow back.

"Ya know," said Russell, "I never could get too excited about ropin' calves but after seein' you ride, I might switch. Wanna buy a riggin'? Only been used *once.*"

It is said that some academics or lawyers relish a good debate and can be quite ferocious, yet it is all done without malice. This story about John could sure be true. . . . I knew his brother.

SEMI-TOUGH

Jack was lamenting the way pro rodeo had changed. He said in the old days it attracted a "less sophisticated" participant, though certainly a more colorful one! Back in the days of six-and-a-half-foot bareback riders and bronc riders, who drank the champagne and ate the glass!

He told me a tale about a Montana cowboy. He told me several tales, but this one is fit to pass along.

John was big, slow talkin', and easy to entertain. He'd been workin' his way home and had made a hundred miles in two weeks. This particular afternoon, he was passing time in a cowboy bar in Whitehall.

A tourist came into the bar and ordered a beer. Since John was the only other patron, the tourist slid over and opened the conversation. "Whyn't we push arms for a round?" John looked at the big ol' boy and drawled, "By gosh, sounds good to me."

They put their elbows on the bar and clasped hands. John thumped the tourist's hand on the bar so hard, the cigarette fell outta the moose head's lips!

"I wuddn't ready," complained the tourist as he looked at his bleeding knuckles. "Let's do it again."

"By gosh," says John, "sounds good to me."

This time, John bent the tourist's wrist into the shape of a G and flattened his class ring!

"How 'bout a finger pull?" challenged the good-natured tourist. "By gosh," says John, "sounds good to me."

They locked fingers, and John jerked him off his bar stool and outta his Acme stovepipes!

"Maybe you'd like to rassle for a round?"

"By gosh, sounds good to me."

John thrashed the poor feller around the bar, tipping over the pool table, breaking the front window, and scattering chairs all the way to Three Forks! Finally the puffing tourist raised a protesting paw, and John released him. There was an 8.20 x 15 tread imprint on his forehead and a tooth mark on his right ankle where John had chewed through his boot!

"Do ya box?"

"By gosh, sounds good to me."

The tourist squared off in time to see a big fist at close range. He went backwards like a bent sapling, sprang back, and took a left cross in the other eye.

The tourist stood there with two black eyes, a bloody nose, sawdust stickin' to his sweaty back, and nothin' left of his shirt but collar and cuffs!

"I guess I better be goin'." The tourist smiled and offered his hand.

John shook it and said sincerely, "By gosh, if ya ever git back . . . stop."

This is not a bar like T.G.I. Friday's or Hooters, where you can get designer beer and put it on a credit card. They don't take checks or have a dartboard. Either one would make it too easy to commit a felony.

MIDNIGHT AT THE OASIS (BAR)

"It's midnight at the Oasis, and I've been here since nine . . ."

The Oasis Bar, perhaps you'll recognize it. It looks like this: gravel parking lot, cinder block building, bars on the windows. A neon sign with at least three of the letters working at any given time and the inevitable palm trees. You walk up to the door and there's a sign on it that says USE OTHER DOOR.

"Everyone's still in their places. I know 'cause I'm still in mine . . ."

You walk around to the other door. There's a sign on it that says WATCH YER STEP, and there ain't no step! As you press through the door into the cozy surroundings, you notice that one of the regulars has stuck a cigarette butt in the moose head's lips and the hair has worn off its wattle. There's duct tape on the pool table, KWITCHURBELLYAKIN behind the bar, blue spots on the ceiling, and a guy asleep under the shuffleboard.

"The pickin's ain't great . . ."

Pinto and I wrote a song called "Midnight at the Oasis (Bar)." It's about the kind of place I described. We figured it was highly unlikely that Barry Manilow or Madonna would cut it, so Pinto did. It's hard for non-big-timers to get the radio play necessary to sell records, so we decided to promote his classic honky-tonk song another way. We would send a copy of the record to every Oasis Bar in the Western Hemisphere. They could put it on their jukebox.

". . . but they never were . . ."

So I wrote a friendly letter to the Liquor Control Board in every state capital, asking for their computerized list of Oasis Bars and their addresses. The response was overwhelming! More than forty states wrote back and wished us good luck. Plus friends and folks have been sending us addresses of Oasis Bars in their hometowns.

". . . out here where the buffalo roam . . ."

Eleven P.M., elbow-deep in barflies, beer dryin' on yer lap, seven dollars wadded up in yer shirt pocket, and hope in yer heart. If you've been there, this song is dedicated to you.

". . . and it's midnight at the Oasis, and nobody's goin' home."

O sis Ba

Although I have logged many thousands of miles on airplanes in coach crisscrossing the United States and also Canada, I rarely go overseas. I'm not sure how much sense this story makes, but it describes my mental numbness.

JET LAG DIARY

This huge draft horse of an airplane takes off from the Sydney airport. Australia, not Nebraska. It's too big to be real. It's like a *Popular Mechanics* prediction. I have no idea how it flies. Magic, the flight attendant said.

I have deprived myself of sleep last night in an effort to trick my body clock. I set my watch to Colorado time. One-thirty P.M., Sydney time, becomes 9:30 P.M. the night before. At midnight, by my watch, I doze off . . . for four hours. My eyes itch, my muscles ache, and my brain thinks it's noon!

This morning I woke at 4:00 A.M. I lay there waiting for the sun to come up. By 5:00, I was out in the driveway, diggin' up an electrical wire I'd buried with the water line to Dionicio's casita. It is in a trench five inches wide and four feet deep! By 6:15, I was back inside and called everyone I could think of who might be up. They weren't!

Last night, I dozed off during supper. I'm dreaming Australian dreams. Kangaroos stick up out of the tall grass like young boys wearing Mickey Mouse ears. We top a dirt track doing 70 kph to find the road filled with sheep! I'm trying to adjust to the weightless stirrups of the Australian stock saddle.

STILL WAKING UP AT 4:00 A.M.! I find the shorted-out splice in my buried wire about 5:30 A.M. I walk down to the pasture to check on the two ol' cows left to calve. I think I see a kangaroo on the slope above the creek. By 3:00 in the afternoon, my eyes are burning and my brain is mush! I vow to stay awake till 10:00 P.M. By 6:00, I'm asleep in my chair.

Tonight I'm tellin' my poetry to the cowboys in Clay Center. It's hot. We're all sweating. My body is fighting my memory for control. I forget a line.

Last night, I dreamed I was laying in the muck with my arm up a cow, trying to bring the calf's malpresented head around. The two Australian vets who had generously offered to allow me to show 'em the "American way" were solicitously bracing my feet and encouraging my efforts. I woke with my right arm tangled in the sheets and my wife standing beside the bed with a surprised look on her face!

I slept twelve hours straight! Woke up at 11:00 A.M. It's suppertime now, and I'm still goin' strong. Maybe I'm back on track.

After giving some clear-headed thought to my jet lag problem, I've concluded that it's no wonder I was in such a state. I spent so much time down under, all the blood ran to my head!

I never really thought about the muckety-mucks who play polo as being cowboys, but after riding a mile in their jodhpurs, I'm convinced they are.

THE POLO CLUB

"*. . . The game was so terrific that ere half the time was gone / A spectator's leg was broken just from merely looking on.*" So wrote Banjo Paterson in his famous Australian poem, "The Geebung Polo Club."

Sounds pretty rough, I thought as I drove up to the Denver Polo Club for my initiation. I'd played cowboy polo, which is like playing croquet with hand grenades. But real polo had to be different.

Pictures in the polo magazines showed aristocrats drinking champagne and charging San Juan Hill. Advertisers included Rolex, Mercedes Benz, and hotels in Switzerland. I glanced down at my chinks and Wranglers, suddenly conscious that my jodhpurs were in the laundry! I was thankful that I had worn my official R.M. Williams Australian stockman shoes.

My first concern was that I had never in my life sat in an English saddle. My second was that I was as left-handed as the AFL-CIO.

John, the owner of the club, assured me I had nothing to fear. He was raised in Iran, where polo originated, and was masterful and patient. I was mounted, a mallet strapped onto my right hand, and fed to the lions. The other players swallowed me up and kept me in play much like hockey players would treat a puck.

Although John shouted instructions and amended the bylaws continuously, I learned the most important rule: Keep moving! The crucial concept to understand in polo is *the line of the ball.* If you are driving the ball down the field, no one can cross that imaginary line between your mallet and the ball.

They can, however, bump you off the line, or hook your mallet with theirs. Hooking is akin to swinging a bat at a baseball and hitting a brick wall instead.

My right-hand dexterity showed itself over and over as my setup shots careened at ninety-degree angles between my pony's legs. Defenders merely waited behind me to steal the ball. I would ride into the fracas tilting drunkenly and circling like a man with one oar. I sustained one good blow to the cheek and managed to bloody the ear of one of my teammates.

But I didn't quit. I was spurred on by the rule that read, "If a rider gets thrown, the play continues if he is not in the way." Same for a broken mallet. In the case of a broken ball, the largest piece shall be played.

". . . And the Cuff and Collar captain, when he tumbled off to die was the last surviving player so the game was called a tie."

But let me tell ya, it's a cowboy game! It's fast, it's a'horseback, and it's thrilling. And I'm gonna try again when my shoulder joint heals and I can borrow some jodhpurs. Wonder what size Prince Charles wears? He's bound to be in the phone book.

Kelly is one of my veterinary colleagues. A grand storyteller in his own right, and I've done my best to recount his bizarre and harrowing tale. It has to be true; nobody could make this up.

KELLY'S HALLOWEEN

It was a bad day at Black Rock that fateful Halloween.
It all began the week before. The call had seemed routine.
"I've got a mare needs checkin', Doc.
I b'lieve the sweetheart's bred."
"I'll swing by there this afternoon," Good Doctor Kelly said.

The mare was mincing round the stall as Kelly donned the sleeve.
"This should only take a second." His assessment was naive.
"She's just a little nervous, Doc, but . . . I guess I would be, too.
If you were pointin' that at me, I'd kick you to Timbuktu!"

Which is precisely what she did. So fast it was a blur.
The next day poor ol' Kelly wore a cast from hip to spur.
With two days off the heal up, his left leg plasterized,
He volunteered to take a call. I know it wasn't wise.

But you know men . . . like him I mean, a grad of Colorado
Whose head, if not for gristle wouldn't even cast a shadow.
Another horse. A small wire cut there just below the hock.
"He's gentle as a newborn lamb. He'd never hurt you, Doc."

And sure enough he blocked the site, though awkwardly, I'd think.
He had to spread his legs the way giraffes bend down to drink.
Relieved, he got his suture out, assumed the bent position
About the time a fly appeared in search of fly nutrition.

HAPPY HALLOWE
BOB BLACK'01

And lit upon the horse's foot. Just fate I would suppose.
The pony kicked to flick the fly
but caught the doctor's nose. Sideways.
Which left a thumb-sized piece of schnozz now dangling from the tip
Like half a jalapeño flapping down upon his lip.

Thirty stitches . . . on the outside. Then they taped that sucker tight.
But them M.D.'s must've chuckled 'cause that bandage was a sight.
It stuck out like a gearshift, like the fruit on prickly pear,
Like a big white avocado on a chain saw grizzly bear.

He stayed at home the next two days, hibernating in his cave
Until his wife had asked his help. The instructions that she gave
Were "Pick the kids up right at nine at Johnson's, Second Street.
They're at a party, Halloween. Maybe you could trick-or-treat."

"Very funny," Kelly fumed. But when nine o'clock came around,
He wedged his cast into the truck and drove himself to town.
When they let him in the Johnsons' house
he matched the decorations.
The kids all froze. Then screamed in fear and heebie-jeebie-ations!

"The mummy! No, it's Frankenstein! It looks so realistic!"
With crutch and cast and nose and scowl it dang sure was sadistic.
But the scream that topped the evening off was,
in Mr. Johnson's view,
When he grabbed and jerked the bandage off and said,
"Hey, I know you!"

When this commentary ran on National Public Radio, there were several listeners who objected to my "blatant endorsement" of the Lands' End jacket. In my defense, no money changed hands. It's just a good jacket, and I said so. Oddly enough, if it had been a bad jacket, I'd have told the story and never mentioned their name. For those who are concerned about how horses do in our part of the country, southeast Arizona, aka God's own brierpatch, it is surprising to me how seldom they get injured beyond the occasional sticker. They slide through the thickets like dolphins. The only thing sticking out on the horse is you!

BRUSH JACKET TESTIMONIAL

A year ago, I was approached to do a testimonial by an upscale environmentally conscious maker of urban clothing named Lands' End. Since neither Wrangler, Resistol, Bailey, Copenhagen, or Coors had ever called, I figgered it was better than Uncle Billy's Baldness Salve or Depends.

I told them I would consider it as long as the product was biodegradable, herbivore friendly, and barbecue proof. They sent me a catalog, with instructions to pick anything I wanted.

I chose a brush jacket. They didn't call it that, but that's what it is. Brush jackets are insulated and made out of canvas like wagon tarps, tents, or Carhartts. These jackets are the standard uniform in cow country, where mesquite thickets and other equally thorny, prickly, spiny, daggery menaces await the dedicated cowboy. To maintain my own credibility and give it a fair endorsement, I put it to the test.

At the next roundup, I donned my new jacket to gather cows with the crew in the dreaded Parson's Pasture. I started in the lower arroyos, riding through two miles of mesquite, dagger yucca, ocotillo trunks, and crucifix thorn tall as a low windmill. It got so thick, my horse was on his hands and knees trying to find the trail.

Malicious thorns the size of pitchfork tines pierced my boot tops, my rhinoceros hide chaps, and my galvanized wrist cuffs. Catclaw big as the talons on an eagle hooked and pulled at every piece of leather, flesh, or cloth that was exposed, leaving thousands of horizontal slashes and scrapes, shredding my tapaderas into ribbons, and spinning my rowels till they got so hot they set my boots on fire.

Then we chased some cows out of a cholla forest—wicked cactus over the horse's head that breaks off, clings to you, and works its pins and needles through your clothing and into your skin. When you clear the forest, rider, horse, and cow are festooned with bratwurst-sized cholla chunks like Christmas ornaments on a hirsute manatee.

Then, just for the sake of product integrity, I rolled through a pineapple field of barrel cactus, lay on the cattle guard, and let two loaded twenty-foot stock trailers back over me slowly, was drug through a wet field of corn stubble by two three-year-old colts, and lay underneath a '69 Ford pickup while they changed the oil.

The results of my test? Lost one button. A remarkable testament to the durability and toughness of their great brush jacket, which I guess allows me to keep it. That should help compensate for the burnt boots, melted spurs, shredded chaps, and thirty-five stitches. I only wish we could have found my other ear.

I was accosted by a politically correct e-mail vigilante after this NPR commentary ran. She accused me of picking on a black athlete. I asked why she thought he was black. She said that "yo," "bro," and "gorilla" were racial stereotypes. I asked her what was wrong with him being a black athlete if the story was true. I asked if she was black. She said yes. I asked if she thought I was black. She said no, she didn't think so. But she just assumed. I asked if she had assumed the cowboy was black. No, she just assumed he wasn't because she didn't know any black cowboys. I offered to introduce her to some. We parted amiably.

THE COWBOY AND THE ATHLETE

Robby eases by, tradin' and trainin' a few horses—doin' day work and helpin' out. He lives in a cow-college town with a pretty good rodeo team.

An Adopt-a-Horse carnival came through town, and Robby wound up being asked to "train" a mustang bought at auction by a local dentist. The purchase was a six-year-old stallion, fourteen hands, woolly as a grizzly and wild as the last Bramer steer to be gathered in the fall.

Robby castrated the stud and went to work. In six weeks, he could actually ride the snake around in the pen.

For his first public outing, Robby decided to saddle two horses and lead Root (as in "root canal"). It was a weekend, so he chose a path across the college campus to introduce Root to some new sights and sounds.

Bebopping across the grass came what appeared to be an athlete. Broad shoulders, bald head, sweatpants, and tennis shoes the size of bass boats.

"Yo, bro," saluted the full-ride scholarship recipient, "I shore feel like a horseback ride!"

Robby looked him over. He was a finely tuned specimen of years of grooming, coaching, bodybuilding, brainwashing, and confidence building. He had YEA, THOUGH I WALK THROUGH THE VALLEY OF THE SHADOW OF DEATH, I WILL FEAR NO EVIL FOR I AM THE MEANEST GORILLA IN THE VALLEY! on his T-shirt.

"Sure," said Robby. "Lemme help you up."

Root was skittish but the "Meanest Gorilla" crawled up in the saddle. The stirrups were just right. He took the reins.

"Try to stay on the grass," suggested Robby, "in case you fall."

"Fall! Humph!" was the reply.

Well, to his credit, he didn't fall. . . . Instead he flew, possibly even glided, soared . . . maybe *catapulted* would capture it best. Root made two good leaps, then drove his front feet in the ground and fired the Gorilla over his head like a navy jet being launched from a carrier, nose first directly into the sea.

He scraped a streak of dead grass off the hard lawn three yards long with his forehead when he skidded to a stop.

Robby caught Root and rode back to the scene of the accident.

"I believe you can ride him, bro," said Robby. "Climb up and try again."

The athlete pondered the possibility, fingering the two pieces of his eighty-five-dollar wraparound sunglasses.

"Maybe later," he said. "I think I heard the bell."

"OK," said Robby. "Anytime."

"Yo," said the Gorilla.

"Yo," said Robby, who hadn't heard the bell. Mostly because it was Saturday.

The cattle business is one of the riskiest businesses one can be in. Worse than professional gambling or having a peach orchard. Many of the examples could be extrapolated to fit "Twenty-five Things Akin to Robbing a Bank with a Putty Knife" or "Twenty-five Things Better Than Smallpox."

TWENTY-FIVE THINGS LIKE BEING IN THE CATTLE BUSINESS

1. Knowing the thrill of victory and the agony of defeat
2. Being handcuffed and forced to watch someone butcher hogs on your living room carpet
3. Parking your new pickup at the end of your driveway, knowing it will be stolen by morning
4. Playing poker with Donald Trump, Al Capone, and Bruce Babbitt
5. Being the public relations manager for Ted Turner, Ted Kaczynski, or Ted Kennedy
6. Being Bill Clinton
7. Watching a train go into a tunnel that you know is blocked at the other end
8. Going to Del Rio for Cinco De Mayo and taking your cross-country skis
9. Going to Las Vegas with a twenty-dollar bill and no return ticket
10. Two-man bungee jumping with your banker, while the cattle buyer holds the other end of the line
11. Getting teargassed and enjoying it
12. Losing the $6 million lottery by one number

13. Buying stock in Chernobyl the day before the fire
14. Discovering you're related to Saddam Hussein
15. Walking a tightrope across the Grand Canyon
16. Seeing your face on a dartboard at the regional IRS office
17. Finding out that the FBI and *Earth First!* have you under surveillance
18. Receiving news that your rich old bachelor uncle died and left his entire estate to the Newfoundland Dog Foundation
19. Discovering that the only way your assets and liabilities could balance is if you married Bill Gates
20. Going to a barber and saying, "Be creative!"
21. Playing pool on the kitchen table
22. Losing your brakes at the top of Wolf Creek Pass
23. Getting your prostate checked six days a week
24. Having a drought break with a seven-inch downpour that washes away your home
25. Being bitten by your own dog

Harold paid his debt to nature and left it like he found it. How many of us will be able to say that? It's easy to be green when it's not personal.

BACK TO NATURE

Harold has been dismantling his feedlot. He built it in 1951 and eventually achieved a 30,000-head capacity. You can imagine the accumulation of steel, rubber, railroad ties, nails, car bodies, pipe, chains, wire, horseshoes, and baler twine. He has completed most of the hauling off and is ripping the ground that has been packed like roadbed. He's planted it to millet. He is returning the land to its natural state.

Harold's reason for razing the feedlot is, of course, urban encroachment. The land is too "valuable" to raise livestock on it.

In the next few years, Harold's feedlot will become part of the city. Crisscrossed with tile, cable, wire, iron, and asphalt. It will be drilled, scraped, paved, disemboweled, pounded, and polluted. Millions of tons of concrete, brick, timber, glass, and iron will rest in or on old feed alleys and sick pens. Oceans of sewage, mountains of refuse, and purgatories of poison will work their way into the soil upon which the city is built. It will become the receptacle for the waste of human herds.

Ancient civilizations as mighty as ours have disappeared. All that remains of them are the ruins of the cities: the Aztec and Egyptian pyramids, the great walls, the foundations of majestic coliseums and castles. But it is hard to find the ugly footprints of olden agriculture, a hog wallow, a horse corral, the trail to water, the milking shed, an irrigation canal, an overgrazed pasture, the chopped-down woods. They seem to have vanished.

I think the reason for this is that, though agricultural production changes wide expanses of land, the changes are not deep.

If you want to look at long-lasting destruction of the environment, you need go no further than any major city. If people were to abandon Washington, D.C., Atlanta, Chicago, Denver, or San Francisco, how long would it take the earth to heal the scars left by man? How many years after abandonment would we still see pieces of the Golden Gate Bridge, Denver International Airport, or the Empire State Building? Hundreds? Thousands? Compare that to the time it would take a cleared pasture, a clear-cut forest, or a highly fertilized irrigated desert to return to its natural state.

It has always bothered me that a self-proclaimed environmental lobbyist can point from his high-rise and accuse ag producers of destroying the environment. It's truly the pot calling the kettle "non-green."

Whether we live in town or in the country, we all play a part in the degradation of our environment. We eat the bounty of modern agriculture. We drive to and fro and we buy two-by-fours.

By dismantling his feedyard, Harold is doing more than most of us to allow the land to return to its natural state. However, the next squatters on the property may leave a more long-lasting legacy of destruction.

The earth is constantly trying to heal the scars on its skin. But we humans just keep pickin' at the scab.

A little run-of-the-mill drama.

THE MOVE

She stood in the kitchen of the manager's home. She and I and the manager's wife. She fidgeted, seeming unsettled, uncomfortable, unsure, and a little scared, perhaps. Through the kitchen window, I could see the U-Haul van with a ten-year-old pickup in tow. She and her husband had just driven eight hundred miles so that he could start a new job. She was worried about where to put her dog.

As I looked out the window, I remembered the times in my life when that was *my* U-Haul parked out front. New job, new town, new boss. It was exciting! I had been anxious to get started!

Her husband felt the same way, I guess. No sooner had he landed than he jumped in the new boss's pickup, and they drove down the feed alley toward the mill. He looked as exhilarated as a kid at Christmas! Three weeks ago, this feedlot owner had sought him out and offered him the job as mill manager at a healthy raise in pay. There is nothing better for a man's ego except possibly an old sweetheart who jilted you getting fat.

As an afterthought, he shouted back to his wife, "See ya in a minute!"

Back in the kitchen, I stood watching this woman . . . a stranger in a new land. You could hear the page turning in her life. She would remember this day forever.

It occurred to me that how she was treated in the next few days would determine how good an employee her husband would become.

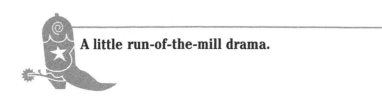

She had not given one moment's thought to the size of the broiler, the number of front-end loaders, the condition of the elevator pits, or the grain on hand. She was worried about their nest. She needed to define her territory.

She would mentally note if the furnished company house was clean. If the carpet was in good shape, if there were water spots on the wall, if the appliances were old or new. If there were places for the kids, the dog, and her plants.

In the first week, she'd find out what kind of people her husband worked for. Would they fix the broken showerhead? Would they replace the torn curtain in the kids' room?

If they treated her like baggage, she would protectively conclude that they didn't appreciate her husband, either.

How important do you think her opinion is? Do you think it is in her power to make her husband go to work a happy man? Or, on the other hand, to make his life miserable?

I was jogged from my reverie by the manager's wife's voice: "I know you're tired from travelin' all day, but I imagine you'd like to take a look at the house we've got for you. We've just redone the bathroom. . . . Oh, and bring the dog."

You could see the change in her eyes.

COWBOY CURSES

- May you be trapped in an elevator for twelve hours with a family of eight who just finished a big meal of fried cabbage.
- May you get bucked off ten miles from camp on the only day you decide to ride barefoot.
- May the BLM decide your hay meadow is good goose habitat.
- May your son join a vegetarian commune.
- May your sheep pay for your cattle operation.
- May the *Western Horseman* magazine run the dude's picture instead of yours 'cause he looks more like a cowboy.
- May you discover one of the barn cats missing after you've butchered rabbits.
- May it rain two inches the day after you sell your cows.
- May your only TV appearance be on *60 Minutes*.
- May you jerk your slack just as the steer drops off a fifty-foot embankment.
- May you sell your calves the day before they go up ten cents a pound.
- May a Wyoming sheepherder offer to buy your best bull to feed his sheepdogs.
- May you cough at the wrong time in the sale barn and buy twenty-six head of broken-mouthed Shetlands.
- May the drought break the day you cut your hay.
- May the chore boy use your good rope to stake the milk cow out in the bar ditch.
- May your only good dog get caught in the neighbor's hen house.

- May your blue heeler bitch get settled by a Pekingese.
- May you notice your missing wedding ring as you put the last scoop of wheat in the elevator.
- May your daughter get engaged to a fifty-six-year-old biker.
- May the local gossip discover your Jane Fonda workout video.

FIFTY WAYS TO FOOL YER BANKER

There must be fifty ways to fool yer banker. I woulda made the loan payment but . . .

1. The cow I was countin' on had a heifer calf.
2. The racehorse I bought missed the turn.
3. The price of hogs went up, so I bought more.
4. The price of hogs went down, so I bought more.
5. The Miracle Fence business tapered off.
6. I shot the wrong cow.
7. Amway wasn't all they told me it was.
8. My gold mine petered out.
9. Ma bought a new pair of overshoes.
10. My modeling contract was canceled.
11. Somebody stole my calender.
12. The weather was too hot (13) cold (14) dry (15) wet.
16. My dog ran off to the neighbors.
17. I lost my calculator.
18. My daughter got married (19) pregnant.
20. It was you or my tire man (21) vet (22) bookie.
23. I overslept.
24. I had a vision that said, "Wait!"
25. You looked like you didn't need it right away.
26. I paid up at the Elks Club instead.
27. I lost my wallet (28) your address (29) my mind.
30. Avon came calling.
31. I had a flat (32) mental block (33) baby.
34. The cat needed an operation.
35. I joined the marines (36) foreign legion (37) hippie commune (38) Baptist Church.

39. I spent it on sympathy cards to my other creditors.
40. I invested in racing greyhounds.
41. I gave at the office.
42. They only let me give blood once a week.
43. I renewed my subscription to *Livestock Weekly.*
44. I bought a lamb at the 4-H sale.
45. I repainted the FARM FOR SALE sign.
46. My horse went lame.
47. My pickup was repossessed.
48. My tractor caught on fire.
49. My topsoil blew away.
50. My dreams went up in smoke.

I admit I'm skeptical of economics being called a science. I've always sort of thought a Ph.D. in economics was the equivalent of an astrologer getting her name in the Yellow Pages. I have many friends engaged in the profession . . . but then I have friends in prison, too. All I can do is be there for them when they are paroled.

ECONOMIST NIGHTMARE

I have always been mystified by the study of economics. I have friends who in every other respect seem to be intelligent, practical, plainspoken, credible people, not prone to astrology, soothsaying, or betting the horses. Yet, they practice the art of economics, yes, even calling themselves *economists.*

If auctioneers go by the title Colonel, lawyers by Esquire, and bawdyhouse managers by Madam, what is the proper title for admitted economists? Oracles? Surmisers? Enigmatists? Fudgers? What do they call the economist who graduates last in his class? Wrong!

I've had a recurring nightmare wherein I graduated with a degree in ag economics. Norwest Bank and Wells Fargo had no vice presidential slots open and Farm Credit had filled all its loan officer spots with retired county agents. In my dream, I am forced to hang out my shingle and advertise my services:

BAXTER BLACK . . . ECONOMIST . . . ANALYSIS & CONJECTURES
By the book, by the number, or by the hour

Each week in this dream, I write a column called *Bluffing with Bax: Theoretical Vacillations on the Market.* The following is a sample:

The sheep market is down again for the 357th consecutive week, due in part to the restrictions on imports of Colombian wool, which lacks the proper density to resist cigarette burns, and the dreaded Panamanian ked.

To maintain your position in this downward market, sheepmen are encouraged to look forward to better times, should they ever come, by making friends with the Peruvians who seem to have a ready supply of herders, yet no experienced ovine therapists. Which is in itself a contradiction.

The relationship between the falling price of corn, cattle, oil, timber, and copper and the rising price of cornflakes, steak, gasoline, houses, and police salaries continues to defy Newton's Third Law of Economics, which says, "Gravity has no effect on consumer markets except when it does." It is an immutable, indelible constant that I adhere to most of the time.

As for the future of the hog market, there is no doubt that it will remain in disequilibrium as long as consumer demand, import regulations, corporate lobbying, and producer sacrifice remain stable.

And so it goes in *Bluffing with Bax*. That's it for this week, and you can take that to the bank!

I believe people have a right to make well-informed bad decisions. Subsequently they should have the character and self-respect to live or die by them. It is called taking responsibility. Ladies and gentlemen, it's the cowboy way.

TOBACCO SUITS

The Marlboro Man has his hands in the air. Several state governments are holding him at gunpoint demanding . . . what? Money, of course. What does government always want.

As this robbery is taking place, we seem to be watching a movie in which the audience knows where the microfilm is hidden but the actors have had their brains removed. Is tobacco addictive? Have smokers known this since Pocahontas lit up John Smith? Is this a secret?

We as a nation have taken care of our cancer-plagued, coronary-prone, emphysematous victims of this vice. Just as we take care of those who succumbed to the lure of other temptations and suffered their consequences—marijuana, heroin, AIDS, whiskey, greed, cocaine, and disingenuous gurus.

So why sue just the tobacco companies? We are not suing Ernest & Julio Gallo or the brokers who promote speculation on soybean contracts or the TV preachers who ask for your last farthing as a love offering. They damage at least as many lives. But the suit is not about justice or retribution. It is about money. The root of all evil.

The plaintiffs doing the suing have managed to circumvent the tobacco company's strongest defense strategy, i.e., the warning printed on the package right in front of their eyes that says, *Don't smoke, stupid.* The victim's justification is "I couldn't help myself. The devil made me do it. It's not my fault. Pay me."

So they spar around until government and the lawyers all agree on their share of the loot. Then it will be settled.

But we can take comfort in knowing that as soon as the Marlboro Man has had his pockets picked, Joe Camel is mugged, and Virginia Slim is assaulted, the lawyers will be looking for other prey.

As a matter of fact, recently a suit was filed against the dairy industry by a lawyer for a client claiming he was addicted to ice cream. They were particularly adamant about demanding warning labels.

WARNING: *Consumption of almond mocha fudge satin ripple ice cream by people who have the self-discipline of a pack of wild dogs can lead to premature love handles.*

If he wins his suit and warning labels are put on ice cream, the dairy industry will have to beef up its promotion to overcome it. Course, their timing is good. I know at least three advertising symbols that may be available soon. The Marlboro Man might look good with a milk moustache.

THE DREADED BLUE BOX

I had just finished loading 184 seven-foot steel T-posts, old ones, by the way, in my pickup and was unloading a mere twenty-four bales of hay from the front section of my gooseneck stock trailer. It was a hot, humid afternoon in early fall when the dead branches begin to stick out of the cottonwood greenery, and the garden starts goin' to hell and no one cares. I could almost smell the cumin from Ramon's #6 Combination Plate being distilled in my sweat from lunch earlier. Then I saw the blue box.

The dreaded blue box. It was still in the stock trailer. It needed to be moved.

The blue box is a metal toolbox I have had since I bought my first set of "made in America" wire cutters, thinking they would last longer. I have now realized that all wire cutters have the sharpness longevity of fresh fruit. They should be thrown out about as often as you empty the trash barrel in the shop.

Anyway, over the years, the blue box has become my chain holder. It will hold four or five good log chains. I have always said that a hundred pounds of salt weighs more than a hundred pounds of anything else. But a ten-by-ten-by-eighteen-inch metal toolbox full of log chains is harder to carry than a sheet of plywood in a hurricane.

There are other things that can stimulate a similar sinking feeling, e.g., the same cow prolapsing for the third time, somebody commenting that my horse seems to be favoring his left front, or the bedside phone ringing in the deep of night.

I don't know exactly what it is about the old blue toolbox that I dread. I've heaved it, moved it, loaded it, dropped it, pushed it, and cussed it through a lifetime succession of jobs and homes, horses and kids, and ups and downs.

Maybe it's not because it's heavier than God's own anvil, clumsier than an ostrich in a Porta Potti, or uglier than a '58

Buick. No, maybe it's because I realize it's gonna outlive me by a long time.

By its earthly clock, I'm just a temporary passerby, while it will still be here when men are walking on Pluto.

I have thoughts of storing my chains in a gunnysack, takin' the ol' toolbox to the dump, and reestablishing the peckin' order in my life. But every time I get as far as step one, I see it lyin' there like a concrete loaf of bread, like a two-hundred-pound rattlesnake, and the dread sweeps over me in a wave.

So, I let it lie or move it if I have to. I've come to realize there are some things you just can't do anything about.

Sometimes I feel a little twinge when I tell a story on a friend. Will he be embarrassed? Will he hate me? I justify it by giving him a complimentary copy of this book. Egotistical, I know, but if he doesn't like it, he can always take it to the flea market and sell it for a couple bucks.

PETE AT THE ALTAR CALL

The Lord works in mysterious ways.

Pete is one of the pillars of any community. He works hard at a hard job, then volunteers his time for civic and church projects. He and his family are musical as well, and share their talent generously. Pete is also devout and regularly attends the Baptist Church.

The spearhead, bomb site, bull's-eye, yea, even the purpose of a Baptist church service is the altar call. The chance to accept Christ and be saved. It is also a time for those already in the fold to come forward and renew their vows or pray.

Pete had been working the late shift and pouring concrete on the side. He was doin' his best, but it was wearin' him out. During the altar call, he felt the need to seek guidance.

He stepped out into the aisle and came forward. After acknowledging the preacher, Pete knelt beside the podium and began silently praying. He prayed through the first verse. Then the second. The third, and finally the fourth stanza of "Softly and Tenderly." The preacher glanced discreetly to his side to see Pete kneeling—more accurately, slumping, in prayer.

The reverend indicated for the song leader to continue singing, so great was his respect for this righteous brother. The congregation changed to "Jesus I Come" and began again. Granted, some in the crowd were fidgeting.

Somewhere during the course of verse four, one of Pete's kids slipped to the front and shook her dad's shoulder. So deep was his peace, he had fallen sound asleep shortly after kneeling and melted into an unapproved cross-legged lotus position. Pete stirred, looked up like a deer in the headlights, and attempted to stand. With a self-conscious nod to the preacher, he stumbled back down the aisle, lurching from side to side, grasping, then shoving off from pew to pew. He fell into the seat beside his wife as the organ hummed its last note.

Pete doesn't remember the singing much, but he has a distinct memory of being alarmed that he must have been struck by some mysterious crippling illness for his irreverence. Of having no sensation below the knees.

It was only when he glanced at his feet, as he pinballed down the aisle, that he noticed he was walking on the sides of his shoes, leaving tracks like a seasick roller-blading orangutan.

However, he was pleased with himself in retrospect that he had remembered to wipe the drool off the altar step below his chin before rising.

I'm always a little suspicious of the folks involved with fanatical organized do-goodism; they seem to have no sense of proportion.

WHALE DILEMMA

Oh, what a Solomon's dilemma. Oh, what a two-edged sword. Oh, what a politically correct Pandora's paradox.

The confrontation included no easy villain. The cast featured animal rights activists, self-proclaimed environmentalists, Native Americans, and whales. All representing themselves to be spokesmen for Mother Earth's best interest. Except the whale, of course, which was the baby presented to Solomon.

The Makah Indians of Washington State claimed a treaty right that had been granted them by the U.S. government in exchange for their land. We gave them a small reservation, some beads and blankets, and the right to hunt and fish without having to buy a whale stamp from the Fish and Game.

The tribe was forced to quit hunting whales with a canoe and harpoon after the United States, Russia, and Japan decimated the whale population to the point of extinction with nuclear warheads and dynamite (small exaggeration, but you get the point).

The whales rebounded and were removed from the Endangered Species list in 1995. The Makah nation planned a hunt.

The professional activists organized and hounded the Indians. But strangely enough, they were unable to muster sufficient outrage from the whale-loving public. Which is most of us, I guess.

Ultimately, it appears our feelings of guilt for the Native American's plight was greater than our guilt for the whale, so we stood by and let the tribe harpoon one.

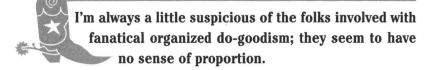

Those defending the whale raised an appropriate hue and cry: ". . . A horrific tragedy. It's just the beginning. Anybody who thinks it stops here is dead wrong. It is really the shot heard round the world!"

". . . One hundred and fifty years ago, it was for food," said one activist about the tribal hunt. "Now it's for fun."

To the tribe's credit, they did it the hard way. Literally with harpoons and canoes. But I suspect there won't be a flotilla of tribal harpooners taking to the water. After all, what are you gonna do with it after you drag it to shore? How much work would it be to butcher a carcass that weighs as much as a loaded Kenworth? And who can you give twenty or thirty tons of blubber to? I'll bet it's harder to give away than zucchini.

I expect that in the end, the Makah folks will not make much of a dent in the whale population. After all, how many head mounts can you hang above the mantel.

I've got a lot of admiration for outfitters and hunting guides. They remind me that we have contemporaries living amongst us who know what pre-Columbus Indians knew. Tuned into nature in a way most don't even have a glimpse of. My hats off to them, and Big Eddie, too.

HUNTING CAMP COOK

Fall is hunting season. Airports from Bozeman to San Antonio are filled with men in camouflage suits carrying gun cases out of Baggage Claim. They are here to stalk the fleeting deer and the wily elk. And, they bring with them millions in revenue, part of which winds up in the pockets of outfitters and guides.

Good hunting camps do much to attract hunters, often year after year. Some camps are elaborate, others Spartan, but all boast a good cook.

Hank's brother Dan ran a guide service in the Big Hole. He enjoyed much repeat business due, according to other outfitters, to his reputation of having the most entertaining camp in western Montana.

The star of the Big Hole Wilderness Experience and Wildlife Procurement Extravaganza was Big Eddie, a puppy-hearted pit bull/Power Wagon cross. At six foot six, 280 with a full beard, he took up a lot of room in a two-man tent. He was officially the camp cook.

There was a natural hot spring near the camp. Dan had tapped this resource by installing an eight-foot stock tank in the spring, thus creating the only hot tub on the mountain. One twilight, a member of the hunting party came in dog tired. He swung up the trail to the hot tub, anticipating a good soak before supper.

Unbeknownst to him, Big Eddie was basking in a little hot water therapy. As the hunter stumbled into the clearing, Big

Eddie rose to his full height, shedding water like a three-hundred-pound buffalo robe, and covered himself in surprise! The frightened hunter wheeled, and ran into camp screaming there was a grizzly bear in the hot tub!

On another occasion, Big Eddie had stayed in camp during the day to watch the sourdough rise. From his tent that morning, he spotted a nice cow elk ease into a clearing near camp. Eddie grabbed his gun, chambered a shell, and stepped through the flaps. His dangling suspenders caught on the upright and jerked him over backwards. A shot rang out! The propane tank exploded! The supply tent caught on fire, disintegrating a pack train full of expensive, down-filled, waterproof, brand-name, guaranteed, color-coordinated, Davy Crockett–recommended, eco-approved, nothing-under-three-hundred-dollar stuff. Not to mention a couple of Weatherby rifles.

But despite his frequent Boone and Crockett screwups, Eddie had a way about him that reminded the visiting hunters that they were in the presence of a primitive force.

Eddie served stew one night. The whiner of the group stirred it with a spoon and then griped, "I don't like carrots." Big Eddie bent over the petulant hunter. He took the plaintiff's fork and picked the carrots out of his bowl one at a time, and ate them.

"There," he said.

2001
©

My son, Guy, read the part of the three-year-old when this appeared on NPR. He did it well. . . . Of course, he was three at the time.

WEE THANKSGIVING

How do you explain Thanksgiving to a three-year-old?

"A long time ago . . ."

"Yesterday?"

"No, more than yesterday. A bunch of people came in a big boat . . ."

"Pirates?"

"No, good guys and mamas and babies . . ."

"And boys, too?"

"Yup, and boys, too. But when they got in the woods, they were hungry but they didn't know what to eat."

"And they had bears in the woods, and tigers."

"Probably, but they didn't see them. So they were hungry and walked around looking for something to eat. And then came the Indians who lived in the woods."

"With . . . with bows and arrows and shooting?"

"No, no. The Indians said they would help them find something good to eat . . ."

"Like fruit bars and Pop Tarts and chickanuggets . . ."

"Well, the Indians said they should have a picnic, and so the Indians got some turkeys to eat and they cooked 'em and made fry bread and corn on the cob . . ."

"But no peas, but some cottage cheese and bread and honey . . ."

"Right, so they made a big table . . ."

"On the blanket . . ."

"Yeah, no table, just a big blanket, and they all ate and ate till their stomachs were full . . ."

"And the little boys, too?"

"And the little boys and little girls and little boy and girl Indians, all of 'em ate . . . and then took a nap."

"But the little boys no wanna take a nap. Little boys wanna play with bows and arrows."

"Okay, but when everyone woke up, they were happy. So the Indians shook hands, and they all said Thanksgiving to each other and Thanksgiving to God . . ."

"And to Jesus and Pastor John and Grandmother Phyllis and to all the little boys."

"Yup, and they said it was so much fun, let's do it next year."

"And tomorra or free days."

"So now every year, we have Thanksgiving with friends and eat a lot and say thanks for the blessings we have."

"Bessing? What looks like, a bessing?"

"A blessing? Sometimes it looks like a little boy."

"Like me?"

"Yup, sometimes it looks just like you."

Barbecued *cabrito* is traditional southwestern fare; they raise a lot of Spanish goats in west Texas. Rarely do they travel by air.

GOAT DAY

I had invited several friends to have Thanksgiving at my house. (A tradition my insurance agent says I can no longer afford.) Each of my guests were gracious and had asked if they could bring anything. When Mac asked what he might contribute, I suggested he bring the goats.

"Goats?" he asked.

I explained that Friday was Goat Day. We always built a big fire outside and spent the afternoon basting Spanish goat in sop made from Shiner's beer. And, since the best Spanish goat came from west Texas, I figgered he could bring it.

"But I'll be flyin' my own plane," he sputtered.

"Perfect," I said. "They'll only be in transit a short time."

Although he did his best to talk me out of it, I remained firm.

So that fateful Tuesday morning, he was out on the San Angelo airport tarmac takin' the backseat out of his twin-engine Bonanza. The ever-vigilant Drug Enforcement Agency noted his suspicious behavior and took him in for questioning. His truthful explanation was so preposterous that they called me in Colorado to check his story!

Upon his release, he flew to Junction, Texas, and picked up four Spanish goats. He hog-tied each one and put them in gunnysacks, which he taped around their necks. Sort of a goat-head bota bag. He spread newspapers and scattered straw just in case.

Four hours later, Mac was swingin' wide around the busy metropolitan Denver airspace, in touch with the Stapleton International tower. The goats were in full chorus and bleating each time he keyed the microphone.

"This is twin Bonanza . . . baa . . . baa . . . four-zero . . . blat . . . blat . . . seven-three . . . bleat . . . whiskey . . . braaaack. . . ."

We were waiting at the Tri-County Airport when Mac dipped his wing and skidded down the runway. He crawled out on the wing. I noticed his hair was standing on end. He looked like he'd been castrating pigs in a metal building. You could almost hear his ears ringing. His eyes were glassy, his voice hoarse, and he was vibrating.

I opened the passenger side to the deafening chorus. The imprisoned smell of four enclosed goats hit me head-on. The floorboard carpeting looked like Walden Pond.

Goat Day was the highlight of that Thanksgiving, and Mac got proper recognition, but his plane was never the same. On hot west Texas afternoons when he planned to go flying, he would spray Lysol, scatter sliced onions, and sprinkle Old Grandad and cooked cabbage in the cockpit to mask the scent. It never worked.

No matter what he did, after riding in the plane for an hour, he would smell like an army of goats had adopted him and marked him as their personal territory.

He eventually sold the airplane at a yard sale . . . on a cold winter day.

THANKSGIVING

My idea of a vegetarian meal is a turkey sandwich. Course my idea of a salad is a jalapeño and Miracle Whip. I've been told my eating habits would make a hyena bulimic. I eat mostly meat and candy.

But I look forward to Thanksgiving. My fondest Thanksgiving memories span a six- or eight-year period after I got married back in '83. Bein' a single late-thirties cowboy type at the time of the wedding, I had become frayed around the edges and was hangin' with some equally frayed late-thirties cowboy types. The kind of people you would not normally have in your home on a holiday.

I convinced my darlin' that it would be charitable to have these misfits at our house for Thanksgiving week. I made a good case for their neediness. I read from Matthew 28:12. I promised to replace anything that did not survive the week, from shrubbery to furniture to goldfish. I even offered to have the in-laws for Christmas. She agreed.

Our invitations went out and were received like a leg o' lamb at a coyote reunion. They came from all points of the cowboy globe, from Idaho, Colorado, Wyoming, Nebraska, and Texas. They arrived by plane, pickup, Amtrak, Greyhound, and thumb. They were well behaved, in the sense that a herd of bison would be well behaved at a faculty wives' tea. But they tried not to cuss around the kids, leave too many bottles and cans behind the furniture, or track mud and snow on the livin' room rug.

I've never been to Planet Hollywood, Studio 54, or the locker room of the World Wrestling Federation, but I would guess Goat Day was close.

On Thursday, we had turkey, company, music, and awesome good cheer! Friday, we sacrificed goats in the snow and barbecued *cabrito* outside in the frigid Colorado air, toasting our good fortune.

And I spent Saturday and Sunday tryin' to get 'em all to leave.

This Thanksgiving, I sit down at a nice table with calmer, more sedate company. We stuff ourselves, and afterwards, sit around and talk about the bad habits we quit.

Course some of this more sedate company are veterans of Goat Day. Older but no wiser, just treating themselves a little easier. I like it just as well, and I don't have as big a mess to clean up after. Happy Thanksgiving to you all.

I have the good fortune to be surrounded by friends like Freddy and Robin, and we are all blessed that our friend Ken is a lawyer who does cowboys pro bono. If the intricate legal details of this story evade you, imagine how the judge must have felt.

FREDDY'S TRIAL

Ken took Freddy's case for the same reason ivory poachers, Enron, and Billy the Kid are able to get legal assistance: morbid curiosity.

"It's open-and-shut," explained Freddy. "See, I hired this man to artificially inseminate my cows. I should have been suspicious when he gave me such a good deal on the semen. I'd never heard of the breed, but the price was right. A month or so later, I put in a cleanup bull. Kind of a Poland-China cross with a big swollen foot like he'd spent the winter in a bear trap.

"They were due to start calvin' on Labor Day. Nothin' happened for several weeks. Then they started poppin'. All the calves were spotted and had one clubfoot! Direct descendants of the cleanup bull. I figger none of the A.I. breeding worked, so I'm takin' him to court."

Ken collected the gruesome details and stressed the importance of establishing the actual calving dates. This could be compared to the A.I. man's breeding dates, which would show that none of the calves were a result of the artificial insemination. Unfortunately, Freddy's extensive records had been lost when he cleaned out his glove box.

Freddy fairly leapt with excitement! "I have a witness who was there at Thanksgiving!" He'd seen the baby calves and could vouch for their age at the time. "Very young," Freddy said seriously.

The day of the trial, Ken put Freddy on the stand to present his case.

In anticipation, Ken had schooled Robin, Freddy's loyal friend and star witness, about his testimony. First, they must establish his credibility as a stockman, more than just a casual observer of the livestock business. Second, they had to relate his visit to Freddy's ranch with a specific date, mainly Thanksgiving.

Robin took the stand and was sworn in. He sat, turned to the judge, and raised his left hand, displaying a missing middle digit. "Roping injury," he said solemnly. Then he winked at Freddy as if to say, "Credibility established."

Ken led the witness like a hung-up bareback rider. "And was there any special reason the date of your visit to Freddy's ranch remains so vivid in your memory?"

"Yes, your honor," said Robin sincerely. "It was a beautiful afternoon, we were riding through Freddy's cow herd. It was shortly after a meaningful relationship had gone awry. I was riding a new horse that I'd been given by a close personal friend. I was suddenly transported to my youth, a family time when my uncle, God rest his soul, returned from the war. He let me ride in the saddle in front of him. I was full of the love, adulation, and childish pride to be there with Uncle Tony. It was so vivid a recollection, there in the midst of Freddy's sleek and peaceful cows, my eyes brimmed like a fountain and I was taken back in time. I could almost taste the turkey and jalapeño gravy." Robin wiped a tear from the corner of his eye.

"And approximately what date was it?" asked Ken.

"Labor Day," said Robin, "I remember it like it was yesterday."

"Case dismissed!"

People who "love" machinery are handy to have around. After all, there are some things that are difficult to do a'horseback.

DOZERMAN

Ron is one of those good ranchers who has an affinity for machinery. The new bulldozer was his proudest possession. The monsoon rains had turned his northern Mexico ranch as green as Indiana. But they had also washed out a few pasture roads.

He kissed his wife good-bye and headed out the door to spend the day "dozing." She handed him his lunch sack and commented on the new straw hat he was wearing. "All you need is a cape and mask, and you could be 'Dozerman,' " she teased.

Well, Dozerman had a great day. He smoothed, graded, and moved large rocks *in a single bound.* At day's end, he started home. Passing under a dead oak tree, he noted that, being *more powerful than a locomotive,* he should push it over someday.

Little did he know that his superthoughts were being monitored by residents of the oak tree. They mobilized and swarmed the open cab of his bulldozer. Attack of the killer bees!

Dozerman was unprepared. The air around him was filled with angry buzzing. Little squiggly feet, flapping wings, and pointy stingers tormenting his ears and arms and head and knees. With cartoonlike martial arts flailing he managed to knock his new hat onto the dozer track. He caught a glimpse of it riding forward and disappearing over the front like a log going over a waterfall.

Seizing control of the situation, he leaped from the seat, arms windmilling. He tugged his hat from beneath the track and, being *faster than a speeding bullet,* he tried to outrun his attackers.

In his mind, he imagined diving into a lake to evade the swarm. Alas, there was no lake. They continued to dive-bomb his hair, neck, and torso, to crawl down his collar and into his gloves. He rolled, whirled, pirouetted, stumbled, skipped, and cartwheeled across the pasture, slapping himself silly with his free hand and beating his hat into the shape of a dish towel.

Finally he outran the horde and stopped, arms on his knees, chest heaving. He looked back through his swollen vision to the bulldozer still purring like a mountain lion under the oak tree. How had he run the course of rocks and knee-high weeds without stepping on a rattlesnake?

And, how does someone, even with X-ray vision, find his glasses when he can't see them? Undaunted, he waded back the way he had come, swishing the deep grass with a big stick like some demented beachcomber, and got lucky.

The bees had won the round, but they let him sneak back on the bulldozer and clank home in his flapping straw turban, crooked eyewear, and bumpy skin. He was a sight to see.

Look, up in the sky, it's a bird, it's a plane, no . . . it must be Dozerman's hatband and right glove being carried off to buzzard heaven.

Battle scars . . . some are more glamorous than others.

THE BULLRIDER'S LIMP

When I was a kid, we had what we called the "bullrider's limp." If you were entered up the Saturday before, you could develop a limp and make it last for a week! When a good-lookin' sweetheart asked what happened, you kinda shuffled and shrugged it off. "Got hurt," you'd say. "How?" she'd ask on cue. "Ridin' bulls," you'd explain nonchalantly.

Images of John Wayne, stoic and brave, filled the air. The dragon slayer injured saving the damsel. The concerned female dabbin' peroxide in the bullet wound creasing your shoulder. "It's nuthin'," you'd say, wincing in pain. If only you had a saber slash across the cheek.

I remember when George and I went to the Bare Ranch for a week. We worked and sorted the cows, checked the bulls, and helped the crew finish up the fall work. On the last night, George was injured in the line of duty. He wore a cast for weeks, explaining every time he was asked that he'd hurt himself working cows. When pressed for details, he'd finally admit he'd broken his ankle when he fell off the cookhouse steps!

Jess's injury was not as glamorous and harder to explain. It looked like he'd been snorting raspberries! His nose was the size and color of a ripe plum.

"Lissadig to hib xplane id wass hart to keeb a strate fase." He'd picked up a bale of hay to feed the heifers. With the practiced motion of experience, he'd hefted the bale and dropped it over his upraised knee. But here the story takes a different twist. The baling wire broke! It struck like a snake, whipped around, and bit his nose!

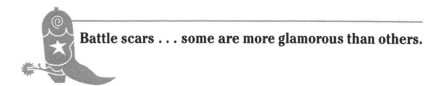

The end of the wire penetrated the meaty part of his proboscis on the left side, drilled through the nasal septum, and exited his right nostril! With a climatic flourish, it wound a dally around the other end of the wire!

His daughter and wife looked on, dumbstruck! Jess grasped the wire and cautiously moved it side to side. His head flopped back and forth like a hypnotized chicken! While his daughter ran to the shed to get some wire cutters, his wife, Shalah, unwound the wrap and tried easing the wire back through the entry hole. Jess stood like a twitched horse getting his mane roached.

He stayed out on the ranch for quite a while, tryin' not to blow his nose and packin' it with ice in the evenings. However, even in their remote ranch country, word spread. They had a steady procession of neighbors coming by to offer sympathy and get a firsthand report. That way, they'd have credibility when they told the story over and over and over. . . .

HIND SPEAK

"Hey, buddy, maybe you'll rope better after your horse foals. Ha, ha!"

"Thanks, pal. I had a horse like yours once. But his brain was so small, his head caved in and he bit his own ears off! Look, it's starting in yours. . . . See that indention."

The quick retort. That clever comeback, the snappy rejoinder that puts the annoying smart mouth in his place. The French call it *esprit de l'escalier*—"the wit of the stairway." In my case, it would be better called *esprit de l'much later.* I don't think of what I wished I'd said till I'm tossing and turning at two o'clock in the morning.

My normal response to the roping chide would have been more like "Huh? Oh. It's a gelding. Yeah, I guess you know, I get it. Ha, ha. Duh!"

The trick is to let the tormentor step into his own trap.

"My gosh, Bill, if I had a bull that threw calves like that, I'd sell 'im as quick as I could!"

"You had . . . you did. I bought him at yer yearlin' sale two years ago!"

"This is ridiculous havin' to nearly undress to get through airport security."

"I've never heard anyone say that who's been hijacked."

"I've been tryin to call you for three weeks to tell you about this great networking investment opportunity. How do you expect people to get ahold of you if you have an unlisted phone number?"

(A visual *esprit de l'escalier* . . . the raised eyebrows.)

"How can you live without a computer?"

"Somebody's gotta think up all that stuff you read on that little screen."

"Ugh . . . how can you wear that fur coat?"

"I'm doing research on lunatics, and this seems to be good bait."

"Dear, why do you always undercook my bacon? You know I like it crisp."

"Yer mother always cooked it crisp, and she said you were difficult to potty train. I don't want you to revert."

"I hope you don't mind us joining you. Looks like yer catchin' all the fish."

"Not a bit, have y'all been vaccinated for leprosy?"

"Would you mind me cutting in line? I have a handicap."

"Oh. You a Republican?"

"I run every day. Are you familiar with running?"

"Yeah, I saw The Fugitive."

"Don't feel bad; you can't be good at everything."

"All I'm tryin' to do is zip this jacket."

"How could anyone be so stupid?"

"Maybe it's the company I keep."

Now that you've got the idea, try this on. . . .

"Did you make that bridle yourself, or is your kid learning leatherwork in kindergarten?"

Marvin Garrett is a World Champion bareback rider and the horse "Try Me" was his equal. She actually bucked so hard, she lost her balance and "went down," but she recovered so fast, she appeared to shoot straight up out of the ground. How she did it, I'll never know, and how Marvin hung on is beyond me. It wasn't pretty. It was astounding.

TRY ME

When Marvin Garrett nodded his head, no one knew that eight seconds later Thomas & Mack Arena would be covered with goose bumps.

Marvin drew Try Me in the fourth round at the National Finals Rodeo in 1989. He marked her out and hung the steel to 'er like the rods on a Union Pacific driver! Try Me jumped the track! She slid, slipped, and rolled around inside her skin! She punched holes in the arena dirt!

Somewhere in the last two seconds, Marvin reached his limit. Everything in his firebox—experience, intuition, talent, and training—were at full throttle and blowin' blue smoke! It was then, over the din of 15,000 rabid fans, Marvin reached down inside himself. I heard him whisper, "Yer mine. . . ."

The hair stood up on the back of my neck. The buckin' horse went down! From where I sat sixty rows up, it looked like Marvin's shoulders actually hit the ground! His legs pistoned! The horse exploded! She climbed out of the hole with Marvin stuck to 'er like a remora on a shark's back.

I don't believe you could've cut Marvin loose with an acetylene torch.

The whistle blew. The crowd went wild! Marvin tipped his hat. But if you'd touched him at that moment, it woulda been like layin' your hand on an electric motor. He was hummin'!

Marvin had ridden Try Me with all he had left: will. Will, want to, gumption, grit, whatever it is that allows housewives to lift cars off babies and Samsons to pull down temples.

The crowd waited nervously for the score to be posted. We were nervous because of a loose brick in the façade of rodeo rules that says hard-to-ride horses don't always score the best. Most of us in the arena that night would have been disgruntled but not surprised if Marvin's ride had scored out of the money. Style often counts more than difficulty.

But rodeo is not like making a centerpiece out of angel hair and glitter. We're talkin' about a horse that can buck you off and a cowboy that claims she can't. That's how rodeo began, and that night at the National Finals the judges didn't forget it.

Marvin and his pardner, Try Me, scored an 82 . . . good for top money in the go-round. They deserved it.

Six-year-old inquisitiveness.

IS THERE REALLY A SANTA CLAUS?

"Dad, is there really a Santa Claus?"

"Why do you ask?"

"Jason's brother said there isn't. He's in the sixth grade."

"What do you think?"

"I think there is . . . but how does he know what I want for Christmas?"

"You write out a list and send it to him, don't you?"

"Yes, but if every kid does it, how does he ever read them all?"

"Maybe the moms and dads help Santa get some stuff."

"Like if he runs out of Legos at the North Pole, they can just get them at Target?"

"Maybe that's how it works sometimes."

"Or maybe he's just too busy to make them all himself."

"I do know moms and dads can tell Santy if the boys and girls have been good for goodness' sakes and have not been selfish and know the real meaning of Christmas."

"I do. About Jesus being born and Mary and Joseph and the manger."

"And how it is better to give than to receive."

"I always put out cookies and milk for Santa. That's a gift."

"I think it's more like giving to others."

"To Tío Bob and Aunt Tamara and the cousins?"

"And other kids who aren't as lucky as you are."

"Kind of like us being Santa's helpers."

"Yeah, that's a good way to look at it."

"So how does he find everybody?"

"He must have a map of the world or just know the way."

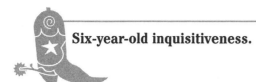

"I'll bet the reindeer know the way, just like Sonny and Coyote know the way home after we're done riding."

"Or maybe Santa has a couple good dogs who ride in the sleigh. They could help him get home, too."

"Like Hattie and Pancho. So, do you think I'll get an Arctic Lego set for Christmas?"

"I can't tell for sure. Only Santa knows."

"Are you gonna get what you want for Christmas?"

"I've already got it."

"Dad, do you believe in Santa Claus?"

"Yep. If you're smart, you'll always believe in Santa Claus."

Dave and Jan are ranchers, but Dave's also an artist (see accompanying drawing) who drives a pickup with a bent frame.

PICKUP DREAMS

I'm not sure what it is about pickups that make men drool. Maybe it's because women drool over men in pickups. But sometimes a cowboy will overreach.

Dave and Jan came by our house on the way to the city. They were goin' pickup shoppin'. "I need one that can handle those steep, rocky canyon roads with switchbacks like a bad case of hiccups and nothin' but washboard between the washouts. It's gotta be able to pull a loaded twenty-foot gooseneck up the face of Gibraltar without grabbin' compound," explained Dave. "I'm thinkin' a three-quarter-ton, four-wheel-drive diesel with manual transmission."

That afternoon, they shopped and shopped. Four big dealerships, each with twenty five to fifty new pickups . . . but not one four-speed manual transmission.

"Everybody wants an automatic," said the dealer.

Dave stuck to his guns, but with each subsequent shiny macho machine he was shown, the sticker price began to weigh heavier on his mind.

He and Jan had dinner in a restaurant, then stopped at one last car dealer. Twenty-eight trucks on the lot. Twenty-seven had an automatic transmission. His dream truck flexed before him. The adrenaline rush surged through him, washing away all budget concerns. He smelled the new grease, felt the gearshift sorta click around the H. He sat tall. He became General Patton leading his cavalry across the Alps.

A couple times the dark cloud of doubt darkened his glittering vision, but Jan encouraged him. "You can do it," she cooed.

They drove it off the lot.

Back home in bed, Dave dreamed of shackles on his ankles. He was carrying the truck on his shoulders as the dealer heaped optional accessories on the bed.

As he wound his way through the next day's chores, he had visions of his children begging on the street, his mother coming out of the nursing home, and his wife selling Tupperware, all to help make the payments. "It's only fifteen dollars a day for six years," the dealer had said. "Just skip breakfast!"

Dave tossed and turned that night unable to sleep. Desperation frayed his mind.

Next morning, the dealer called with a problem. Seems Dave's trade-in had a bent frame. "Can you bring the new one back?" he asked.

Dave gulped, and much to the dealer's surprise, said, "Gas mine up; I'll be there by noon!"

And who says cowboys can't spot a good business opportunity when it hits them in the face?

SALE
4x4
DEAL
"FEEL THE"
POWER
DAVE HOLL

The idle mind is Henry Ford's workshop.

THE FORD EX'S

I was commiserating with a friend a while back who was recovering from a divorce. He had lost his new car. "What kind was it?" I asked.

"A Ford," he answered, "one of the ex's."

"You mean an Excursion, Expedition, or Explorer?"

He said, "It don't matter. Now it's just one of the ex's."

The ex cars, Ford's answer to the Chevy Suburban. But I'm a little worried that their naming scheme is going to play out soon. Excursion? I guess it beats the Ford Hike or Stroll or Ambulation.

They have done well in the past with names: the Mustang, the Thunderbird, the Galaxy, and even the Falcon had a modicum of glamour, but the Expedition? "Let's load up the Sherpas and head for the mall!"

If this pattern continues, will we eventually see the new Ford Excruciate or Exfoliate? "Yes, friends it will take the hair right off your head!"; "Drive the new Ford Explosion . . . but wear your seat belt!"; "Try our new Ford Excuse. . . . If you're late, all you have to do is point to your car: 'That's my Excuse!' "

Specialty cars could be developed for various professions, i.e.,

CONTRACTORS—Excavate
PEST CONTROL—Exterminate
RAILROAD EMPLOYEES—the Extraneous
STRIPPERS—the Exotic, the Exposure, or the Exhibition
MARRIED PRIESTS—the Excommunication
LAWYERS—the Extortion, Extradition, or
the Philip Morris model, the "Exploitation"

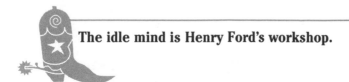

For those who prefer the riffraff to know that the car they drive cost more than a new aircraft carrier, how 'bout valet parking your Ford Extravagant or Exorbitant or the classically simple Ford Expensive?

Many more possible names come to mind that I suspect Ford has considered and discarded or filed away for future use: the Extraneous, the Extreme, the Excelsior, the Extinguisher, the Expectorant, or the Excretion.

Regardless, they build good cars even if they aren't very imaginative, although there are times, as with every make of vehicle on the road, when the owner thinks he's driving a Ford Expendable, a Ford Extinction, or even the ever-popular Ford Expletive Deleted!

CLASH OF THE TITANS

Bernie was a cell phone bully. He was rude and dense and loud.
He was welcome as a cold sore in the midst of any crowd.
He never noticed human beings politely in pursuit
Of contemplation, quiet talk—he wasn't too astute.
He never asked those seated near, "I say, mind if I phone?"
One must assume his boorishness was deep down to the bone.

One afternoon, he strode into the airport waiting room,
Plopped down beside a gentleman that most would say of whom
Was never inconsiderate and normally devout,
But Chuck took on a darker side when Bernie's phone popped out.
He dialed up, then smugly sat, and waited for the call
As if the twenty other folks weren't even there at all.

Then Bernie quick began to blab, his breath to halitose.
His words careened around the room and singed those in too close.
Incensed at Bernie's lack of grace, Chuck gave him quite a start.
Addressed him in a civil tone, "I say, mind if I toot?"
Bernie humphed, then turned away, disdain upon his brow.
"I warned you, sir," Chuck smartly said, then fired one 'cross the bow.

It caught poor Bernie's pinstriped suit and frayed his snappy threads.
The sharp lapels curled at the tip, his collar hung in shreds.
But Bernie felt he had a right to bother and impose,
To force himself on all around. His conversation rose.

Another strong yet subtle blast, an SBD, I guess,
Was Chuck's response, and Bernie took it full upon the chest.

It rose up like a mushroom cloud, encircled Bernie's head.
His words cut smoke rings from the fog—like donuts, people said.
But undeterred by Chuck's attacks, he never took the hint,
He blabbered on like all was fine but he'd begun to squint.
Chuck launched a dank torpedo, an aromatic burst
That set poor Bernie's hair on fire as toxic fumes dispersed.

The phone began to crackle, there was static on the line.
But rudeness is a funny thing, can cloud a person's mind.
He stubbornly refused to budge, remaining quite obtuse.
His tie began to throb and glow, his boutonniere came loose.
Chuck reached down deep for one last blast, achieved his heart's desires,
That cleared the room and left the scent of burning rubber tires,

Of heavy metal meltdown and of twisted steel grooved,
But . . . amidst this flaming ambience ol' Bernie sat unmoved.
His ragged suit lay at his feet, no longer pleats and creases,
Just single-breasted leisure wear, like melted Reese's Pieces.
His tie somehow survived the fight, though wadded up and stained,
But . . . in spite of being scorned and shamed, his obstinance remained.

Chuck's ire was up, still resolute, he'd shown this clod what for,
That piggish manners would not go unchallenged anymore.
They tried to stare each other down, these Titans wound up tight,
One, who'd reached his patience's end, the other, impolite.
Just then ol' Bernie's cell phone rang, though feebly, it is true,
He looked at Chuck, then took the call, then said, "Well, it's for you."

For those concerned enough to worry, we experienced millennium panic. It was as real as most other phobias, i.e., speaking in public, being too fat, or stepping on a crack. It all turned out to be in our mind. It was a high-tech phobia that would never have risen its ugly head if the new millennium had begun in 1965.

Y2K—NO SWEAT

Time is inexorable. Time marches on. Time and tide tarrieth for no man. But time is arbitrary. A clock is the figment of man's imagination. Like musical notes or justice.

How long shall we make a day? What shall we call this birdsong? What would be a fair sentence? We have concocted something out of thin air, built a whole system around it, and chained ourselves to its capricious rules to the point that the world lay in panic at the coming of some whimsical imaginary date called Y2K.

But who says man can't roll back the hands of time. Maybe he can't, but he can dang sure roll back the hands of the clock! He does it every year when he wants to. Daylight saving time, he calls it.

Newfoundland is in a time zone thirty minutes different from Quebec. Madagascar is fifteen minutes from everyone else. The simple fact that you can set your watch ten minutes fast shows that time is no more a real thing in the scope of the universe than the color you paint your house.

So if we were truly concerned about the world coming to a screeching halt the first day of 2000 . . . we could have just changed the numbers. Have a daylight saving century, or better yet, a daylight saving millennium.

We could have gone directly from December 31, 1999, to January 1, 1000. Surely our computers would have been able to distinguish the Modern 1000 with its car payments, bank accounts, Indian treaties, and space shots from the Medieval 1000 with its joustings, burnings at the stake, and virgin sacrifices.

But most important, we would have simply put the problem off. Not unlike the way Congress puts off saving Social Security every year.

But as you can see, the earth has survived our insignificant tempest in a teapot.

To put the Y2K fear in perspective, we should take a lesson from our fellow earth travelers, the animals. What was the impact of the first day of the new millennium on the insect world?

Roger Miller said it best: "Every day is Saturday to a dog."

This was written for the turn of the century

2020

It is the year 2020. I am seventy-four years old. I quit team ropin' last year. Never did win a buckle.

The U.S. Team Ropin' Association kept raising the age limit to tie on. If I could have hung on six more years, I might have finally caught up. They never would put me back to a two handicap. Doin' good at that one ropin' in 1996 cost me a lot!

The Republicans have maintained control of the U.S. Congress since 1994. Bill Clinton was president then. Yup, the same one who appointed himself and his wife to the Supreme Court at the end of his second term.

The Congress has continued to pass conservative legislation. Now all public buildings are "smoking only." Nonsmokers can be seen on windy corners and office loading docks, sneaking fresh air.

The teachers' union (NEA), sheep, and the Cuban cigar have been added to the list of endangered species.

Minimum wage is still $4.75. Workers are flocking to Mexico in search of high-paying factory jobs. Spanish is now an official language.

The balanced budget amendment has never passed. It cost too much to maintain the Star Wars defense system, which stands ready to retaliate should Grenada ever bomb us.

The drive to enforce term limits on the U.S. congressmen and senators was finally put to rest when Congress passed the Thurmond-Byrd "We know best" amendment.

A movement is afoot in Congress to carve past President Gingrich's face on Mount Rushmore. The Redskins (formerly Indians, Native Americans, Indigenous Peoples, etc.) have objected, suggesting Russell Means's head instead.

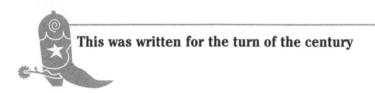

Ted Turner's vast landholdings, including the states of Montana, New Mexico, and Fulton County, Georgia, were recently sold by his heirs to Tyson International meat processors.

The senator from Arkansas, William Jefferson Tyson, has introduced a bill to disallow marriage of practicing vegetarians. In spite of the fact that carniphobia is now considered a disease like alcoholism or Internet surfing.

Puerto Rico is still not a state, nor is Washington, D.C., but Alberta and Saskatchewan are being considered for statehood as I write this.

Global worming has eliminated internal parasites as a cause of concern in pets and kindergartens.

Finally, the cattle business has benefited from the laws classifying feeders and producers and old cow vets with casino gamblers. Therapy is mandated and financed by the Department of Health and Judgment-Impaired Services.

I get a check every month and go to my group sessions. They're all people like me . . . still tryin' to win a buckle. Mostly we talk about the old days.

TOXIC COFFEE

At the convenience store I poured a twelve-ounce Styrofoam cup half full of coffee. Then I put it under the cappuccino–chemical flavor dispenser, and dribbled in French magnesium vanilla, hot cobalt chocolate, and hazelnut ammonium hydroxide. Then I took two each of the pasteurized artificially flavored synthetic Irish creme, amaretto chloride, and mentholated mint in their peel-, spill-, and drip-thimble cups and tried to splash their contents in the ever-filling twelve-ounce cup.

All the while I was preparing my cauldron concoction, my taste buds were leaping in a bud frenzy, doing gumdrop cartwheels and encouraging my salivary glands to wet their pants. Toxic coffee. An exquisite potion. With my admitted weakness for such an unnatural beverage, you would think that I would have some understanding of my children's love for Pop Tarts, with filling like gritty tar on hot pavement and a hard dough reminiscent of unleavened bread. Usually eaten unheated, it is a cardboard and jelly sandwich.

Or how about dried cereal bits formed into the shape of clover leaves, letters, hatchets, pinto beans, bat eyes, or squirrel testicles, dyed algae green or hemoglobin orange and rolled in powdered cinnamon, baby talc, or graphite?

Food preservatives have been essential to man's civilization. Salted, vinegared, dried, smoked, frozen, or lyed, they have allowed us to live between hunts and harvests. But when I see packaged pastry pizza or trail mix with the shelf life of petrified wood, I get queasy.

Not to mention genetic manipulation, which has given us bright red tennis ball tomatoes that would not break on the bat of Sammy Sosa, with a taste closer to carpet fiber than tomatoes.

Mexican mutant strawberries as flavorless as poi. It's what

we've done to chicken, so we can roll it in carbo dust, deep-fry it, and addict our kids, but I digress. . . .

The ultimate toxic invention . . . a fruit roll-up. A flattened sticky hanky-sized sheet of goo. It reminds me of a frog's tongue on the roof of an octopus's mouth. But kids love it! So be it.

Right now I'm sipping coffee made from fresh ground Costa Rican beans in a china cup with real cream . . . and I'm wishing it had a big squirt of pecan caramel caustic cappuccino with a pH of 2. Probably not a good idea though, might take the enamel right off the cup.

HANDY TOASTS AND TRIBUTES

To the Newly Married Couple

May your love have the energy of a litter of puppies, the work ethic of a boat person, the heart of a Mountie, and may it last until they don't sing "Dixie" in Alabama.

To the Entrenched Bureaucrat

As the years have accumulated like mineral deposits on a west Texas faucet, so has your compassion grown thick and inflexible, so that today you stand like a stalagmite, stodgy of foot and narrow of mind. A tribute to tenure, intransigence, and seniority. You have become a statue of yourself.

To the New Ph.D. Graduate

After years of denial, you now stand at the foot of reality. The accumulated anguish, frustration, sacrifice, and financial hemorrhage of all who supported you has hit bottom. You have emptied the trough, your life's work now begins. It is, in a nutshell, time to make yourself worthy of their faith.

To the New Baby

To the newborn, whose name is still wet on the dotted line, whose age is listed as zero, and whose slate is as clear as her fate is cloudy. Today you do not have to lift a finger. You are royalty, Miss America, Queen Bee, the Dalai Lama, Mrs. Roosevelt's Pekingese. You do not know war, poverty, death, or disease. You know only love. Enjoy the moment.

To the New High School Graduate

Congratulations. By squinting through the fog of anxiety, hormones, posturing, and inexperience, you can glimpse a sliver of your future. Even though it is unclear, it is bright because you are standing on the shoulders of your family and friends, your teachers and coaches, and your ancestral community that stretches back to Genesis. And the taller you stand, the brighter it gets. Say thank you.

UNFINISHED THOUGHTS

Let's say you were an arctic explorer and you suddenly got cold feet.

If you can get snowed in during winter, can you get winded in during spring?

When you put hot water in a thermos, it keeps it hot. If you put cold water in a thermos, it keeps it cold. How do it know?

Do fish ever get tired of eating seafood?

It is the truth in humor that makes it funny. That's why there's no science fiction jokes.

I walked by a decorative chunk of petrified tree in a motel lawn. The sign beneath it said 180,000,000 YEARS OLD. How do they know? Did they count the rings?

I heard Mike Wallace of *60 Minutes* fame was asked to teach a course in ethics. Am I the only one made uncomfortable by that?

I used to work like a horse and eat like a horse. Now I sweat like a horse and trim my toenails with hoof nippers.

If you can see twice as far with binoculars, how much farther can you see with trinoculars?

When you tell your buddy, "Scuze me a minute, I'm gonna slip around behind this tree and relieve myself," how do you know it's the back of the tree?

Mom: "You've got your shoes on the wrong feet."
Kid: "But they're the only feet I've got."

You can always spot a cutting horse man by the coffee stains on his chaps.

Giving your horse to a good trainer is like letting a butcher sharpen yer pocketknife.

I can't make myself at home. . . . I live here!

About his hometown; if you know where it is, that's where yer from.

He's not a professional cowboy, he just does it for a living.

If there weren't such a thing as chicken, what would snake taste like?

If pigs are outlawed, only outlaws will have pigs.

When a man says he's not that kind of a guy . . . he probably is.

On medicating the water at the catfish farm, the receptionist asked, "How will they get the fish to drink it?"

Suddenly, nothing happened!

GLOSSARY

Auscultation: the art of listening for things within the body. Usually done with a stethoscope.

Bad (blue) bag: chronic mastitis—an unhealthy udder, as opposed to a defective shopping utensil.

Baler twine: has just about replaced balin' wire as the means of holding bales of hay together. However, this modernization has led to the deterioration of many small repair jobs on the farm for which only balin' wire would suffice. For instance, you can't wire a loose exhaust pipe to the frame with plastic twine.

Black bally calf: commonly a first-generation cross between a Hereford cow and an Angus bull. They are black bodied with a white face.

Banamine: an equine painkiller.

Beef checkoff: every time a bovine is sold in the United States, one dollar is collected by the beef board. The collective money is used for research and advertising to learn about and promote beef as an alternative to whale meat or tofu.

BLM: the Bureau of Land Management is a division of the Department of Interior. Between the BLM and the Forest

Service, they control over one-third of the U.S. landmass. Most of it in the twelve western states. To the extent that the federal government owns 83 percent of Nevada.

Blowouts: an inversion of the cloaca in fowl. Unfortunately, rubber cement is useless in its repair.

Blue heeler: a stock dog. Relies on a high pain threshold and bravado to move cattle. Bites at the heels. If the Border collie is the quarterback, the blue heeler is the linebacker.

Border collie: a stock dog. Fairly universally acknowledged as the smartest of the species for the purpose intended. Favorite of North American and European sheepmen.

Bosal: a nose band, not unlike a halter used in the training of horses. More user-friendly than a bit.

Braymer or Bramer: how you pronounce Brahma, a breed of cattle.

Broken mouthed: an old cow or ewe that has lost all or part of its lower incisors. A natural occurrence with age. P.S., they don't grow upper incisors.

Brucellosis: a disease of cattle and other species that can be transmitted to man. In cows it causes abortion; in humans, undulant fever. A serious problem before pasteurization of milk became universal. Rare today.

Bulldoggin': a rodeo sport officially known as steer wrestling. A cowboy jumps off a galloping horse onto a galloping steer, catches it behind the horns, and with a twist and a flip throws it to the ground. It is a timed event and has no counterpart in the real cowboy world unless it's a bar fight.

Cake-feeding-pickup: a method of supplementing protein to cows in winter. It is fed in many forms: 40-pound blocks, pellets, loose, or in molasses.

Cancer eye: a disease that occurs primarily in cows with no dark pigment on the skin surrounding the eye. The predilection is heritable. Operable if caught early enough.

Capacho: although not defined this way in *The Oxford Spanish Dictionary,* I know it to mean "good friend."

Carhartt: canvas outerwear, particularly good for brushpopper cowboys. Thorns won't tear it.

Chew: chewing tobacco or snuff (i.e., Redman or Copenhagen).

Chinks: shortened knee-length chaps popularized in California and the Northwest.

Cow pucky: one of many expressions used to define bovine alimentary effluent; as in cow pie.

Cow punching: doing cowboy work.

D-4 Cat: bulldozer. Smaller than a D-8.

Drag to the fire: at branding the 2- to 3-month-old calves are worked. The ground crew waits near the fire (which may be a steel branding pot heated with a propane burner) to administer the appropriate procedures. The cowboy a'horseback ropes the 200- to 300-pound calf around the hind legs and "drags him to the fire." Simultaneously they are branded, ear tagged, vaccinated, castrated, and kissed. It usually takes a minute or two, literally.

Feeder: a feedlot animal weighing 500 to 700 pounds, or a person who owns cattle in a feedyard, or owns the feedyard, or one who works on the feed crew.

Feedlot: the less romantic side of the cowboy world. It is where steers (and heifers) spend their last few months eating grain before they become filet mignon.

Fence stay: a four-foot piece of twisted wire that keeps barbwire from saggin' between posts. You may also see stays made from Ocotillo skeletons, straight sticks, pieces of bedspring, or the occasional car axle.

FFA: a high school vocational tech club that represents young people who are interested in agricultural pursuits from landscaping to genetics. It used to be the Future Farmers of America.

Five-buckle overshoes: standard footwear for cowboys in mud or snow. Fits over boots and rises to mid-calf (human). Thus, "five-buckle deep" is a useful unit of measure.

Gaited horse: one that has a natural tendency to travel in something other than a simple walk. Tennessee walking horses, Paso Finos, trotters, Lepizans, and Andalusians, are examples.

Gelding: a castrated stallion.

Gentile: someone from outside my real world . . . an urban person.

Grulla: a color best described as a cross between sausage gravy and a thundercloud.

Halter chain: a short piece of light chain connecting the head stall itself to the lead rope. A picture's worth a thousand words.

Heifer: a young cow, one that has not had a calf.

Hog-ring: a C-shaped metal clip used to attach tags to pigs' ears.

Hog wire: or sheep wire, depending on your part of the country. It is woven fencing with a vertical and horizontal wire crossing at intervals like a tic-tac-toe board. Prevents smaller domestic farm animals from escaping. Will keep a dog outta the garden but not a coon or squirrel.

Horn: in my context, not the kind you honk.

Javelina: a peccary—a wild beast native to the Southwest, often confused with wild pigs. Tough little beasts, not very tasty.

Keds: a wingless fly that is an ectoparasite of sheep.

King Ranch: a 150-year-old ranch in south Texas that developed the Santa Gertrudis breed of cattle and is famous for its horse-breeding program.

Log chain: essential equipment around the farm. Used to pull dead livestock or recalcitrant machinery, heavy feed troughs, or occasionally the wandering tourist vehicle from the ditch.

Owly: a horse that is easily provoked.

Piedmontese: an Italian breed of cattle.

Polled: genetically hornless.

Power takeoff: PTO: a spinning shaft that protrudes from a tractor. It connects to a variety of farm implements and furnishes them power. Like the shaft on an electric motor.

Preg check: to manually palpate the uterus for pregnancy via the rectum. A routine procedure in the fall on cattle operations across the country. Why veterinarians have asymmetrical shoulders.

Producer: refers to farmers and ranchers.

Punkin roller: a small-town rodeo.

Red Man: chewing tobacco.

Red Wings: lace-up work boots.

Roach: a verb—to roach a horse's mane; clipping the mane down to the hide, leaving the forelock and the witherslock.

Romal: one- to two-foot leathers on the end of a set of reins. An attached quirt. Mostly used to slap a chap leg as a noisemaker to move cattle or pacify cowboys.

Rumen: that vast stomach compartment in a cow where fermentation takes place. Can hold up to 400 pounds in a big bovine.

Saddle fork: the front part of the saddle that straddles the withers.

Scour: (v) to have diarrhea. **Scours:** (n) as in "he's got the . . ."

Settle: get pregnant.

Sheep pellet: as opposed to a cow pie, road apple, dog poop, or tiger scat.

Showin' a little ear: a bovine who shows Bramer traits. In this case, big ears. Like saying *Baywatch* is a little racy.

Slurry pit: a big (up to swimming pool size) pit where runoff, manure, factory effluvia, or potato waste is held.

Snotty nose: a critter with a cold or signs of pneumonia.

Stock trailer: usually a barred trailer from 16 to 24 feet, pulled by a pickup and used to move livestock.

Tapaderas: stirrup covers—worn where the brush is thick.

Tarentaise: a breed of cattle, French in origin.

Team roping: a rodeo event where the header ropes the steer's head and the heeler ropes the hind legs. Imitates real-life method of catching and restraining cattle on the open range.

Tune-up: usually a "training session" to get a horse thinkin' right.

U.P.: up north it's the Upper Peninsula of Michigan, farther south it stands for the Union Pacific Railroad.

Vaquero: Mexican cowboy.

NPR AIR DATES

Cajun Dance 6/20/00

A Cold Call 3/1/01

When Nature Calls 6/28/99

Only Ewes Can Prevent Wildfire 1/6/00

Horse People 4/10/01

March Madness 3/7/01

Cave Painting 6/25/01

Springtime Flying 4/8/98

The Butterfly Wedding 7/21/99

Ranchers and Buzzards 4/1/97

Beans à la Black—a Recipe for Trouble 11/9/01

Drawing a Line in the Dirt 2/11/02

The Producer Meeting 8/15/98

Coming Out 3/22/99

Cat Laws 1/8/98

Chick-Fil-A 8/23/00

Nature's Logic 10/5/99

Kids 3/7/02

Homeless Dogs 8/9/00

Ol' Rookie's Flashback 12/10/01

Hispanic Agriculture 2/4/00

Empty Places at the Christmas Table 12/25/01

Kelly's Halloween 10/31/00

Brush Jacket Testimonial 3/29/01

The Cowboy and the Athlete 2/25/00

Economist Nightmare 1/24/01

Tobacco Suits 9/11/97

The Dreaded Blue Box 5/28/98

Whale Dilemma 8/2/99

Wee Thanksgiving 11/28/96

Thanksgiving 11/22/01

Is There Really a Santa Claus? 12/20/01

Pickup Dreams 2/12/99

The Ford Ex's 1/15/01

Y2K—No Sweat 12/28/99

2020 1/23/97

Toxic Coffee 1/25/02

ABOUT THE AUTHOR

BAXTER BLACK is one of the bestselling poets in America. In the tradition of humorists like Robert Service, Mark Twain, and Will Rogers, he examines his corner of Americana and sheds light on the whys and the why nots of humanity.

His job, as he describes it, is to "turn over our sanctimonious stones, locate our flaws and foibles, and wrap them in hunter's fluorescent orange. To nudge that fine line between good taste and throwing up in your hat."

Baxter can be seen "on the road" entertaining the agricultural masses, heard on National Public Radio puzzling the urban intelligentsia, or found in the company of interesting domestic and nondomestic beasts.

He lives in Cochise County, Arizona, amid the cactus and Gila monsters, and runs a few cows. It's not a bad life.

ABOUT THE ILLUSTRATORS

CHARLIE MARSH was born in the midst of the Second World War and was, you might say, a prototype for the baby boomer—not the successful and prosperous model selected for mass production, but the other one. He was born with an inexplicable and unshakeable desire to be a cowboy but with no aptitude for that or any other profession. Relatives with vivid imaginations, thinking they recognized objects in his childish scribbling, in fearful desperation encouraged him along those lines. In retrospect, it was probably not so much encouragement in that line as much as thoughtful discouragement in all others. However these things happen, he became what might by broad definition be called an artist—not the prolific and famous sort, but the other. As for being a cowboy, he has pursued that lifelong ambition with far more enthusiasm and much less success, so that today you might refer to him with equal chance of error as a "cowboy artist."

Fortunately, he is married to a woman whose talent and useful abilities more than cover his deficit. He, his wife, Pat, and her mother, Vade, live on a small farm about forty miles south of Muskogee, Oklahoma, in Briartown, which would be, had its aspirations been so lofty, a wide place in the road.

Between unclogging toilets, painting fences, and hosting events at the Gooding County Fair, **DON GILL** saddles horses and fixes motorcycles for his children, Hailey and Jordan. On occasion he will draw a cartoon.

Don and Denise Gill live in Gooding, Idaho, with their children, their petting zoo of animals, and a stray teenager or two.

★

Like any boy born during the great baby boom in the U.S., **BOB BLACK** yearned to live the American Dream. Alas, due to a fluke in the hospital paperwork, which listed his birth country as Uganda, this dream would be hard to fulfill.

As a preschooler he taught himself to forge a series of ten-day visas using only an old mandolin nut, some coal oil, and a farrier's apron. Spending every spare moment creating documents gave him little time for socializing until, as a senior in high school, he discovered that the average government-issued visa was good for a year or more. Suddenly, Bob was on top of the world! But, at that altitude his nose started to bleed. Even so, his dream came true.

He and his wife, Stephanie, and their daughter, Samantha, make it all happily happen somewhere in the deserts of central Arizona.

★

As a professional domestic bovine management technician, **DAVE HOLL** spends most of his time involved in ag-viro perimeter containment engineering and equine adolescent behavioral therapy. His hobbies include semivintage automotive mechanical perpetuality and drawing pictures.

Dave lives in the bustling suburbs of Klondyke, Arizona, with Jan, his understanding wife.